William Felton

A Treatise on Carriages

Comprehending Coaches, Chariots, Phaetons, Curricles, Whiskies, &c.

William Felton

A Treatise on Carriages
Comprehending Coaches, Chariots, Phaetons, Curricles, Whiskies, &c.

ISBN/EAN: 9783337102548

Printed in Europe, USA, Canada, Australia, Japan

Cover: Foto ©Andreas Hilbeck / pixelio.de

More available books at **www.hansebooks.com**

A TREATISE ON CARRIAGES.

IN TWO VOLUMES.

VOLUME I.

Entered at Stationer's-Hall.

A
TREATISE
ON
CARRIAGES;

COMPREHENDING
COACHES, CHARIOTS, PHAETONS,
CURRICLES, GIGS, WHISKIES, &c.

TOGETHER WITH THEIR PROPER

HARNESS.

IN WHICH
THE FAIR PRICES OF EVERY ARTICLE
ARE ACCURATELY STATED.

By WILLIAM FELTON, COACHMAKER,
No. 36, LEATHER-LANE, HOLBORN.
AND No. 254, OXFORD-STREET, NEAR GROSVENOR-SQUARE.

LONDON:
PRINTED FOR AND SOLD BY THE AUTHOR;
AND BY J. DEBRETT, PICCADILLY; R. FAULDER, NEW BOND-STREET; J. EGERTON, WHITEHALL; J. WHITE, FLEET-STREET; W. RICHARDSON, CORNHILL; A. JAMESON, LONG-ACRE; AND ALL OTHER BOOKSELLERS IN GREAT BRITAIN AND IRELAND.

1796.

ADVERTISEMENT.

THE nature of the subject here treated of, does not require any great share of literary abilities, otherwise the Author is not vain enough to have attempted it: his education and profession effectually debar him from any pretensions in that way; and he therefore hopes, that any inaccuracies in point of style will be overlooked, and if he has expressed himself so as to be understood, is all he aims at.

ADVERTISEMENT.

As the Author underſtood that a number of the Coachmakers, on hearing of his intended publication, had declared their diſapprobation of it in very pointed terms, and as he pretends not to any ability in his profeſſion ſuperior to that of other tradeſmen, he was willing to ſubmit his various ſtatements to their conſideration; and, with that view, wrote a LETTER to twelve of thoſe whom he conſidered as the principal in the trade, from whom, however, he did not receive any anſwer, but which, it is hoped, will ſufficiently juſtify the Author with the Public from having the leaſt intention to injure the fair trader.

COPY

LETTER.

COPY OF THE LETTER

ABOVE REFERRED TO.

SIR,

I TAKE the liberty of acquainting you, that I have completed for the press (which soon will be published) A Treatise on Carriages and Harness: But conceiving that this may be considered as an attempt to injure the trade, I can assure you I have no such intention; and, to satisfy you that I have not, I am ready to submit the different prices I mean to publish, to the consideration of any candid and respectable person whom the trade may chuse to nominate; and if I shall be satisfied that these prices are not fair both to the trade and the employer, I am willing they should be corrected.

I have sent this notice to twelve, whom I consider as the principal of the profession—and, if they chuse to appoint any one to meet me on the business, I have no doubt that every thing will be adjusted to the general satisfaction.

I am, Sir, &c.

(Signed) WILLIAM FELTON.

CONTENTS.

	Page
INTRODUCTORY OBSERVATIONS	xvii
BUILDING — — — —	1
CHAP. I. BODIES —	5
Chariot or Poſt-Chaiſe Body	8
Coach Body	19
Landau or Landaulet Body	22
Landaulet or Demi-Landau Body	25
II. PHAETON, CURRICLE, OR CHAISE BODIES	27
Gig Body	29
Half-pannel or Whiſkey Body	32
Value of Bodies in their naked ſtate	34

CHAP.

CONTENTS.

CHAP.	Page
III. FOUR-WHEELED CARRIAGES	39
Perch Carriage	43
Crane-neck Carriage	53
IV. TWO-WHEELED CARRIAGES	58
Price of Carriages	65
Carving—Obfervations	68
V. IRON-WORK	70
Springs	71
Coach and Chariot Springs	73
Double Springs	74
Gig Springs	ib.
Long-tail Phaeton Springs	75
Scroll Spring	ib.
Grafshopper or Double Elbow Springs	76
Single Elbow Spring	ib
Loop Spring	77
French-horn Spring	ib.
Worm or Spiral Spring	78
Spring Jack	ib.
Price of Springs, &c.	79
Axletrees	81
Axletree-Boxes	82
Common Axletree and Box	84
Patent Anti-attrition Axletreee and Box	85
Patent Cylinder Axletree and Box	87
New Pattern Cylinder Axletree and Box	89

New

CONTENTS.

CHAP.		Page
	New Pattern Axletree, with double Cafe Box	90
	Price of Axletrees	92
	Cranes	94
	Stays	95
	Plates	98
	Sockets or Caps	101
	Hoops and Clips	102
	Bolts, Nuts, and Screws	103
	Rings, Staples, Loops, and Shackles	105
	Joints and Props	107
	Steps	108
VI.	WHEELS	109
	The Patent, or Bent-Timber Wheel	113
	Price of Wheels	114
	Boots or Budgets	115
	Price of Boots and Budgets	119
VII.	PLATFORMS, OR RAISED HIND AND FORE ENDS, AND BLOCKS	120
	Raifed Hind Ends, Pump Handles, and Short Blocks	121
	Raifed Fore Ends or Fore Blocks	122
	Spring Blocks	ib.
	Cufhions and Standards	123
	Price of Raifed Hind and Fore Ends, &c.	124
VIII.	COACH-BOXES	125
	Standard Coach-Box	126
	Salifbury Coach-Box	ib.

Iron

CONTENTS.

CHAP.		Page
Iron Coach-Box	. .	127
Travelling Coach-Box	. .	128
Chaife Coach-Box	. .	129
The Coach-Box Seat and Cradle	.	130
Price of Coach-Boxes, Seats, and Cradles		131
TRIMMINGS	. .	132
Price of Laces	. .	134
Fringes	. . .	135
Price of Fringes	. .	136
Holders and Strings	– .	ib.
Price of ditto	– –	139

IX..THE LININGS AND INSIDE FURNITURE OF BODIES. – – 140

Squabs, Curtains, Venetian-Blinds, &c.

Quantity of Materials ufed for Linings		150
Price of Linings	– –	151
Price of Infide Furniture	–	152

X. HAMMERCLOTHS – – 153

| Oil-fkin Hammercloths | – – | 154 |
| Price of Hammercloths | – | 157 |

XI. PLATED, BRASS, AND COMPOSITION METAL FURNITURE FOR BODIES 159

Door Plates	– – –	160
Door Hinges	– – –	ib.
Door Locks and Handles	– –	161
Private locks	– – –	ib.
Dove-tailed Ketches	– –	162

Glafs

CONTENTS.   xiii

CHAP.		Page
	Glafs Rollers	162
	Buttons or Studs	163
	Price of each	ib.
	Plating	164
	Brafs and Coloured Metal Furniture	166
	Mouldings or Beads	167
	Price of Mouldings, and Scrcll and Tip Ornaments	169
	Frames	ib.
	Price of Frames	171
	Head Plates	ib.
	Price of Head Plates	173
	Real and Sham Joints	174
	Price of Real and Sham Joints	175
	Body Loops	ib.
	Price of Body Loops	176
	Pole Hook	ib.
	Price of Pole Hooks	177
	Buckles	ib.
	Price of Buckles	178
	Check-Brace Rings and Door-Handles	ib.
	Price of Check-Brace Rings and Door-Handles	179
	Wheel Hoops	ib.
	Price of Wheel Hoops	180
XII.	LAMPS	181
	Price of Lamps	183

Reflectors

CHAP.		Page
Reflectors for Lamps	— —	185
XIII. STEPS	— — —	187
Infide Folding-Steps	— —	ib.
Step-Plates and Stops	— —	188
Outfide Chaife Steps	— —	ib.
Hanging Steps	— — —	189
Price of Steps	— —	ib.
XIV. PAINTING, VARNISHING, &c.		191
Ground Colours	— —	192
Picking Out	— — —	193
Varnifhing	— — —	ib.
Japanning	— — —	195
Herald and Ornament Painting	—	ib.
Prices of Painting Bodies and Carriages		200
Prices of Herald and Ornament Painting		201
XV. CHAISE HEADS, WINGS, KNEE-BOOTS, AND DASHING LEATHERS		202
Chaife Heads	— — —	ib.
Wings	— — —	204
Knee-Boots or Aprons	— —	205
Dafhing or Splafhing Leathers	—	206
Price of Heads, Wings, Knee-Boots and Dafhing-Leathers	— —	207
XVI. BRACES, POLE-PIECES, &c.		210
Main Braces	— — —	ib.
Collar Braces	— — —	211
Check Braces	— —	ib.

Safe

CONTENTS.

CHAP.		Page
Safe Braces	- - -	212
Pole Pieces	- - -	ib.
Price of Braces and Pole-Pieces	-	213
XVII. TRAVELLING CONVENIENCIES		215
Trunks	- - -	216
Infide Straps and Laths	- -	ib.
Trunk Covers	- - -	217
Trunk Straps and Belts	- -	ib.
Imperials	- - -	218
Cap and Hat-Boxes	- -	219
Wells	- - -	220
Splinters, or Splinter-Bars	- -	ib.
Drag-Chains and Staff	- -	221
Oiled Covers to the Body	- -	222
Springs Cording	- -	ib.
Tool Budget	- - -	223
Price of Travelling Requifites	-	224
XVIII. HANGING OF BODIES	-	226

INTRODUCTION.

THE Art of COACHMAKING, within this laſt half century has arrived to a very high degree of perfection, with reſpect both to the beauty, ſtrength, and elegance of the machine: the conſequence has been, an increaſing demand for that comfortable conveyance, which, beſides its common utility, has now, in the higher circles of life, become a diſtinguiſhing mark of the taſte and rank of the proprietor.

INTRODUCTION.

The superior excellence of English workmanship, in the construction of carriages, has not only been the occasion of a very great increase in their number among the inhabitants of this country, but the exportation of them to foreign nations, in time of peace, is become a considerable and profitable branch of British commerce.

The coach and coach-harness makers, though professions of a very different nature, are yet so connected and privileged by each other to follow either or both trades, that more than a third part of the present master coach-builders are in fact only harness-makers, whose judgment in the construction of a carriage can go little further than that of a shoemaker; yet these professors, aided and supported by the coachmakers, have always opposed, and still continue to oppose,

INTRODUCTION. xix

pofe, every other tradefman concerned in the manufacture of the principal materials of which a carriage is compofed, fuch as wheelwrights, fmiths, painters, carvers, joiners, &c. either of whofe judgment muft far exceed that of harnefs-makers; and many of whom poffefs a knowledge little inferior to the profeffed builder himfelf.

But thus united, they ftrenuoufly oppofe every new adventurer in the trade, though ever fo well qualified, if not bred a harnefs or coachmaker, and connected with them in this affociation. They (the affociators) have been pleafed to dignify themfelves with the title of *Brights*, and to beftow upon their rivals the opprobrious epithet of *Blacks*.

This conduct has an evident tendency to a monopoly, and, of confequence, is a

difcoudiscouragement to the ingenious and enterprising tradesman, whose talents might otherwise raise him to eminence in the profession.

The coachmaker, as is generally understood, is no doubt the principal in the business, being the person who makes the wood-work: but there are very few professions wherein a greater number of artisans are necessarily employed; such as those already mentioned, as well as several others. From the capacity of each of these to execute their work in a neat and substantial manner, the credit of the coachmaker principally arises: he ought therefore to be well acquainted with the theory of all the different branches appertaining to coach-building—for without such knowledge, he will prove but a superficial tradesman.

The

INTRODUCTION.

The gentlemen whofe fituation in the world enables them to keep carriages, have hitherto been unavoidably deprived of the means of acquiring fuch a knowledge of the manner of building and repairing them, as would enable them to judge when any attempt is made to impofe upon them, either in the original price charged for a new carriage, fuch as their fancy and inclination may lead them to make choice of, or in the neceffary expence that may be requifite to repair the damages it may have fuftained by time or accident. It is therefore intended to exhibit to public view, fuch a diftinct account, not only of the original price of the carriage, and the repairs that may be neceffary, but alfo of the feparate prices of the different component parts thereof, as will enable any perfon effectually to detect or guard againft impofition. It is therefore prefumed, that this Treatife will be of equal advantage to the gentleman who builds a carriage, as the Houfe-builder's Price-book has, by experience proved to be to him who builds a houfe; and as there are many more gentlemen who amufe themfelves in getting carriages built than in building houfes, the utility of this Treatife will be more general. For if a gentleman wifhes to contract with the builder, for a carriage fuitable to his own tafte, in elegance, beauty, and convenience, he will now, by attending to the prices here given, have it in his power to afcertain the price he fhould allow, without the leaft rifk of being impofed upon.

It frequently happens, that gentlemen, when they get a new carriage built, or have their old one repaired, are difappointed both in the appearance and conveniencies

INTRODUCTION. xxiii

veniencies of it. This arises from the orders not being given in terms sufficiently explicit; an inconvenience that will be effectually removed by the Glossary, and an attentive observation of the Plates given in this Treatise; and the tradesman can have no excuse for not executing his orders agreeable to the directions of his employer.

Another unpleasant circumstance, arising from gentlemen not being previously able to stipulate for a certain price, is, that when the bill is presented, though the prices should be fairly charged, yet they are apt to conceive themselves imposed upon, as the amount may exceed what they expected. This frequently occasions litigations at law; and those who may pay their bills without resorting to this disagreeable method, yet retain, though perhaps erroneously, an opinion that the prices are exorbitant; the confequence is, the tradefman fuffers in his reputation, and, perhaps, lofes his cuftomer.

Carriages frequently get out of repair, from the ignorance or inattention of the coachman, whofe peculiar province it is to watch over the leaft injury the carriage may fuftain, and, by an immediate application of the proper remedy, to prevent the extraordinary expence that muft enfue, by fuffering the injury to remain for any confiderable fpace of time unrepaired; befides, many gentlemen are impofed upon by the mifreprefentations of their coachmen, who too commonly attribute the confequence of their own neglect to the infufficiency of the carriage.

A practice has been introduced, and for a long time continued, that the gentlemen

tlemen of the whip receive *douceurs* from the tradefmen employed in building or repairing of carriages, no doubt with the original intention of encouraging the coachman to take good care of the carriage, and preferve his intereſt with his employer. It is very likely, the zeal and activity of the coachman will, in a great degree, be proportionate to the encouragement given him: very extravagant expectations are formed by many; which, if not complied with, are fure to draw the refentment of the difappointed coachman upon the tradefman; and, if complied with, he has no other method of reimburfing himfelf for this very unfair tranfaction, than by charging an exorbitant price for his workmanſhip; fo that ultimately his employer fuffers a manifeſt injury.

It

INTRODUCTION.

If the coachman be honeſt, attentive to his maſter's intereſt, and a tolerable judge of his buſineſs, he will diſcover when *any* repair is neceſſary; and, in ſome meaſure, to what extent that repair ought to be carried; but, if ſwayed by ſiniſter motives, and the tradeſman ſhould happen to be of the ſame complexion, a wide field opens for colluſion between the two, and the proprietor is ſure of being egregiouſly impoſed upon; eſpecially, as coachmakers' bills are generally given in technical terms, not underſtood by their employers. However, the Gloſſary annexed will give a full explanation of them, and enable the proprietor to detect any fraud attempted to be put upon him by this colluſion.

It is alſo an important part of the coachman's duty, to be careful in preſerving the ſtrength and beauty of the carriage under

INTRODUCTION.

under his care. That his mafter may be enabled to judge whether or not he executes this part of his duty in a proper manner, the time a carriage fhould laft, and the expences for repairing it, are afcertained; and, that it may not proceed from ignorance, particular DIRECTIONS will be given in this Treatife, how the prefervatives for the different parts of the carriage are to be applied, fo as effectually to prevent damage by the ignorance, or impofition by the artifice, of the coachman; and that, without a gentleman defcending, in the leaft degree, to any thing unbecoming his fituation in life.

This Treatife is not intended, nor can it, by any means, injure the fair and honeft trader, but will rather be of advantage to him, in fo far as he may charge fuch prices as are fair and reafonable, without the

the rifk of fufpicion; and his employer will always have it in his power to have recourfe to a regular fair-ftated price, either for building or repairing. It will, however, prove an effectual check upon the fraudulent and defigning, by whom the Author expects to be calumniated.

It often happens that tradefmen, in ftraitened circumftances, are induced, for prompt payment, to work upon very low terms, and even, upon urgent occafions, are tempted to perform work at a lofing price; while others, whofe circumftances enable them to give long credit, charge very extravagant prices on that account. A comparifon, therefore, of the different prices charged by two tradefmen, under thefe circumftances, might miflead a fuperficial obferver; but a proper attention to the charges that are made, under the circumftances alluded to, will enable

enable the proprietor to form a proper judgment, upon the whole, whether he is fairly charged ; the length of credit being a material object in varying the charge that muſt be confidered.

There is little doubt but exceptions will be taken to the prices and regulations here laid down, by ſome tradeſmen who may refuſe to abide by them; but gentlemen will be relieved from this difficulty, as there are many reſpectable tradeſmen who will be very happy to be employed upon the terms, which are ſuch as will enable them to pay a liberal price to every artificer concerned in the buſineſs, and to live reſpectably themſelves ; it muſt neceſſarily be preſumed, that the author is well warranted in his calculations, as it involves his own intereſt, as well as that of others of the ſame profeſſion, and who, for prompt payment, can

afford

afford a difcount of five per cent, at leaft.

It may happen, that defigning tradefmen, when they find they can fo eafily be detected in any overcharge they make, in order to elude detection, may give other names than thofe commonly ufed in the Trade (and of which an explanation is given in the Gloffary annexed) to fome of the articles charged in their bill; in fuch cafes, gentlemen may have recourfe to any tradefman in whom they can confide; or to the Author of this Treatife, who will be very happy to receive any commands the public may pleafe to favour him with.

ERRATA.

Omitted in Page 158.

	Common.			Painted.			Patent.		
	£.	s.	d.	£.	s.	d.	£.	s.	d.
Oil-skin hammercloth —	1	16	0	2	2	0	3	13	6

A

TREATISE, &c.

ON BUILDING OF CARRIAGES.

THAT carriages fhould always be built adapted to the different places for which they are deftined, is a rule invariably neceffary to be attended to, for town, country, or continent; not, however, to fuch extremity as to prevent their ufe in either fituation, but to accommodate them as nearly as poffible to each, as a much greater ftrefs is laid upon the carriage in drawing over ftones and channels, than on a fmooth road. This makes it abfolutely neceffary to build ftronger for the town, than if intended for the country only, owing to the general goodness of our roads: it is also neceſſary to build ſtronger for the continent than even for the town, as the badneſs of their roads obliges them to uſe ſix horſes to what, on a well-made road, two would draw with equal facility.

The conſtruction of every carriage ſhould be as light as the nature of the place it is deſtined for, and its neceſſary work, will poſſibly admit; it is folly in the extreme to add a conſtant oppreſſion, by additional weight to the horſes, as the pleaſure of conveyance ariſes from expedition and eaſe, which cannot be effected in a cumberſome, heavy carriage, beſides the unpleaſant ſenſation of toiling the cattle unneceſſarily.

With regard to accelerating the motion of carriages by mechanical powers, nothing new has yet been effected worth much notice. However ſanguine the inventors of thoſe wheel-boxes, for which they have obtained patents, may be, the only advantage, ſuperior to the common, is their containing oil; which will be more fully noticed in its place. A light carriage and fleet horſes exceed every invention of this kind.

A falſe opinion pervades the mind of many people, which is, to build ſtrong, regarding the durability of the carriage in preference to the preſervation of the horſes. Superior ſtrength is effected only by addition in weight of materials; and

and many builders, regardlefs of any thing but their own credit, are ever impofing heavy durable work, by which they eftablifh to themfelves the character of fubftantial, good workmen.

The principal merit lies in building as light as poffible, yet fo as fufficiently to fecure from danger; what a light carriage may lofe by wearing a fhorter time than a heavy one, is more than compenfated by the prefervation of the cattle. It is alfo reafonable to fuppofe, that the heavier the carriage is, the greater the wear will be on the wheels, and a confequent lofs thereby.

Although, in the Gloffary, the technical terms that are made ufe of by the coachmaker are explained, yet this Treatife will be much affifted by a defcriptive reprefentation on plates—1ft, of the naked framings, or fkeletons; 2dly, of the materials with which they are finifhed; 3dly, of the articles for convenience occafionally ufed; and 4thly, of the carriage in the finifhed ftate.

As it would be too prolix to reprefent the great number of carriages that are finifhed in fo many different ways, it will be fufficient to defcribe two of each fort, according to the prefent mode that carriages are built—reprefenting, firft, the timbers, or fkeleton, thereof, for information concerning the different parts, regulated to a half-inch fcale, reckoning a half-inch to the foot.

One circumſtance, unleſs particularly noticed, will tend much to perplex in reading this Treatiſe, viz. the meaning and application of the word Carriage. In the uſual meaning of the word among coachmakers, it is the lower ſyſtem, on which the body, containing the paſſengers, is fixed or fuſpended, and to which the wheels are placed: though, ſpeaking generally of coaches, chariots, phaetons, &c. they are properly called carriages of ſuch deſcriptions; but as the word Carriage will be frequently uſed in both ſenſes, that which partially ſignifies the lower ſyſtem only, will be printed in *Italics*; that in the general meaning of the word, in common letter with the reſt. As all ſorts of carriages are divided into two parts, viz. Bodies and Carriages, they will be treated of ſeparately—beginning, firſt, with the timber-work, which is the entire province of the coachmaker, and on which a great dependence lies, as to the ſufficiency of workmanſhip.

CHAP. I.

ON BODIES IN GENERAL.

THERE are few mechanical structures executed with a greater nicety than this, it being the receptacle of passengers. The principal attention of the proprietor is fixed on the proper finishing of this part, so as best to answer the purposes of convenience and shew. The form of structure depends much on fancy; the size is proportioned to the intention of its use, and regulated by the width of the seat and the height of the roof; and the finishing executed agreable to the conditions of contract. Its timbers for the framings should be of a particularly dry ash, executed with great exactness through the whole; the pannels are of a soft, straight-grained mahogany, smoothed to a fine surface, and fitted or fixed in prepared grooves, or bradded on the surfaces of the framing; the insides are well secured by glueing, blockings, and canvass, to the pannels; the roof and lining, or inner parts, are made of deal boardings.

BODIES.

As no parts of the framing of the body, if well executed, are likely to fail by ufe, a reparation, in confequence of bruifes and other accidents, is all that is to be expected. The pannels generally fuffer moft injury, either from exceffive heat, or bad quality of timber; and great attention is required in felecting good boards for this purpofe, which, if not extraordinarily dry, are fure to fail, by drawing from the grooves, bulging, or cracking, if confined; but though the timbers are good, if the carriage is expofed to any excefs of hot weather, it is a great chance but they will fly; but no difcredit ought to attach to the builder from that circumftance.

The firft fummer a carriage is ufed will prove the fufficiency of the pannels. So foon as they begin to ftart from the grooves, as they moftly will in fome degree, the builder fhould examine, and relieve them, where confined, to prevent cracking. A little drawing from the grooves is to be expected, and is of no material confequence; but if they crack, it will always be a vifible flaw.

As fufficient room in the body makes the feats comfortable, it fhould be the firft object; and the width of the body ought to be in proportion to the number it is meant to contain. Open bodies have this advantage, that three can fit with tolerable eafe on the fame length of feat as would

only

only accommodate two in a confined one. A full-fized feat for a clofe body to contain three, is from four feet to four feet one or two inches; that of an open body, from three feet four, to three feet five or fix inches. This fize is fufficient for two in the clofe, and from two feet feven inches, to two feet eight or ten inches, in the open bodies. The width acrofs the feats is never regular, as the fhape of the body proportions it: but as the ufual fize of both clofe and open is from fourteen to eighteen inches, the height of the feat from the bottom is, in general, fourteen inches; and from the feat upwards, to the roof, from three feet fix inches, to three feet nine inches; the cufhions not included.

For the advantage of height, it frequently becomes convenient to make the feat moveable. This is only neceffary to give freedom to extraordinary head-drelfes. Few people rife above three feet from the feat; fo that, allowing two inches for the cufhions, there is left in the clear, without the head drefs, from four to feven inches.

As the intention of its ufe fhould regulate the fize of the body, fo fhould the fize of the body the ftrength and weight of the *carriage*; and it is for want of attention to this particular, that the abfurdity of a heavy *carriage* to a fmall body, and a light *carriage* to a large one, may be frequently obferved: the confequence, befides the appearance, is, that the heavy body fooner injures the light *carriage*, while, on the other hand, the heavy *carriage* is an unneceffary incumbrance. In this the builder's judgment muft regulate him, agreeable to the fize of the body, which fhould only be contracted end-ways, by which the fide view, fo effential to the beauty of the carriage, is preferved.

SECT. 1.

A CHARIOT OR POST-CHAISE BODY.

THESE bodies differ not in the leaft from each other. The occafion for their ufe only alters their name: by the addition of a coach-box to the *carriage* part, they are called Chariots; the poft-chaife being intended for road-work, and the chariot for town ufe. If intended for poft-work only, the materials are fomewhat lighter than thofe of a town carriage; but, when alternately ufed, fufficiency muft be obferved. The width of the feat, as before obferved, regulates the fize or ftrength of the body. The framings are not required fo ftrong for one or two, as for three perfons. If generally ufed for three, the length of the feat fhould be from four feet to

four

Plate I.

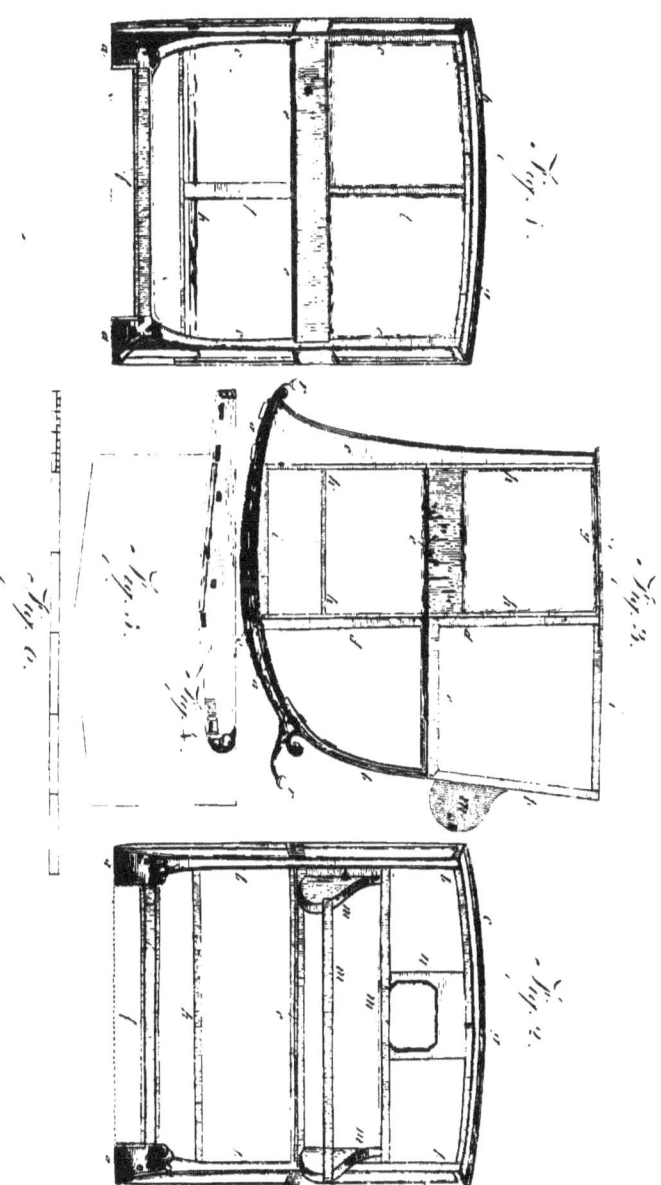

four feet one or two inches; but if only for a third paſſenger occaſionally, three feet eight inches will be ſufficient, with a ſeat to draw out from the centre. The ſize might be reduced, but the appearance would be hurt by it, as a full body looks beſt.

In this ſort of bodies, a greater width is allowed for the front than for the back of the ſeat, to make it more commodious for the elbows; and the door lights, or windows, are frequently contracted on the ſeat-ſide, that paſſengers may be more ſecure from outward obſervation, and, at the ſame time, have a ſufficient view from within. The advantage of lightneſs, alſo, renders theſe bodies preferable to any other; but the mode of finiſhing them depends more upon fancy than others.

To many of the readers of this work, it may be unneceſſary to give ſuch a deſcription of the method of framing. To others, more curious, and particularly to thoſe of the trade who are not ſufficiently informed, it may prove of no ſmall advantage. As the repreſentations on the plates are drawn to an accurate ſcale, it would be ſuperfluous to mention any thing further of the ſizes. That which has already been given concerning the ſeats, &c. for the inſide, is preſumed ſufficient for general notice. Every part of the framing is diſtinguiſhed by name; and the letters againſt each

each will be a reference to the different descriptions afterwards given.

Fig. 1, 2, and 3, are the front, back, and side views, shewing the joints, and the method of framing the separate timbers, previous to putting in the pannels or boardings.

Fig. 4. is the top, or inside representation of the main timber or bottom side-piece, which likewise shews the side-cant, also the grooves and mortices, in which the other timbers are fixed.

Fig. 5. exhibits the angle lines of the body.

Fig. 6, is a half-inch scale of the whole representation.

A. The bottom side, which is the essential or main timber of the whole, as all the rest principally depend on it. It is of a compass make, and forms the bottom line. In it are the standing corner, and fore pillars tenoned, and the steps are bolted on the top. The bottom boards are confined hereto by the assistance of a rocker, which is firmly fixed to the inside. It is also rabbetted from the fore to the standing pillar, for the bottom of the door to lap in, and grooved from the standing to the corner pillars to receive the pannels. The ends are mostly ornamented with a scroll; but sometimes, according to fashion, are left equal with the joints, shewing no ornament.

B. The corner pillar, is compassed on the lower part, and forms the main line or sweep of the body.

body. It is spliced or tenoned in the bottom side, grooved in the side and back from the bottom joint to the middle rails to receive the pannels, morticed at the middle and top to receive the middle and quarter-rails, rabbetted between each for the quarter-boardings, or reduced, if meant for pannels, to lap thereon.

C. The fore pillar, is tenoned also in the bottom side with a double tenon. It entirely shapes the front; and, sideways, it forms a pannel, ten inches at bottom, diminishing upwards. The original surface is sunk, leaving a moulding only at the corner: on this pillar the door hangs, where it is rabbetted to keep out the air. The inside is boxed, or grooved, in separate partitions, for the glasses, shutters, &c. to slide in; morticed in the middle and top for the front top and middle rails, and grooved in front for the pannels.

D. The standing, or perpendicular pillar, tenoned in the bottom side and top rails, is one of the main pillars of the body for strength. It supports the roof in the middle, is rabbetted on the inside for the shutting side of the door, reduced at the lower part for the side or quarter pannels to lap on, which are fixed by bradding thereto. The upper part from the middle is prepared the same way as the upper part of the corner pillars; and in this the seat-rails are also tenoned.

E. The

E. The middle rails, which divide the pannels from the upper quarters, are grooved on the bottom edge to receive the pannels, and rabbetted on the top for the boarding or pannels. They are diſtinguiſhed by the ſituation in which they are placed; thoſe on the ſide, by elbow rails; thoſe in the doors, by middle door rails; and thoſe in the front and back, by back and front rails: the elbow rails only are lapped, and that in the ſtanding pillars; the others are all tenoned in the different pillars. Thoſe rails which form the bottom of the light, or windows, have a ſmall fence reſerved behind, over which the glaſſes, &c. are placed when up, and prevents water from paſſing into the grooves: they are alſo left broad, and ſunk from the original ſurface, leaving a moulding on the top and bottom of the outer edges, forming a diſtinƈt pannel, on which moſtly the creſts are painted; theſe are frequently called door-ſtyles.

F. The two bottom bars, are the moſt eſſential end-framings, and are tenoned in the ends and the bottom ſides; the hind one is rabbetted on the top edge, to receive the pannel, which is ſecured to it by a batten nailed on the inſide; the bottom is grooved to receive the boardings, which alſo are nailed to it; it divides the pannel from the bottom, and is moulded on the outſide. The

fore

POST-CHAISE BODY.   13

fore bar is left level with the bottom furface of the groove in the fore pillar, that the pannel may be bradded on it; a moulding, or batten, is put upon the pannel, fo as to form or imitate the reft of the framings; the bottom is rabbetted for the boardings, which are alfo nailed therein.

G. The roof-rails are compaffed to the intended fhape of the roof, and are denominated as follows: thofe on the fides are called top quarter-rails, which are tenoned in the corner and ftanding pillars, rabbetted alfo on the bottom edges for the boarding or pannels; the door-cafe rails are what form the top cafing to the door, morticed on the ftanding pillars, and its whole fubftance lapped fome length on the quarter-rails, to which they are ftrongly fcrewed. The back and front roof-rails are properly fo called: the back-rail is tenoned in the corner pillars, and rabbetted at the bottom edge for the boardings or pannel; the rabbet in the middle is funk deeper, to receive the board for the octagon or back light, which is made therein. The front roof-rail is tenoned in the fore pillars, and is a framing for the light, the middle of which is deeply grooved out from the bottom, which receives the top of the glafs frames and fhutters when put up; this, with the door-cafe rails, has cornice-pieces nailed on, after the leather on the roof is fixed, which conveys the water from the lights or windows.

H. The

H. The door pillars, of a separate framing from the body, morticed at the two ends and middle for the rails; the one side is grooved in separate partitions, for the glasses and shutters to slide in; the other side is rabbetted, to answer the rabbets of the standing pillars, as they shut in each other, and, thus formed, exclude both water and air; the outsides, from the bottom of the middle rails downwards, are reduced to the thickness of the moulding and pannel, the same as the standing pillars, as upon the door pillars the pannel is fixed, and a brass plate is screwed to the side of each with a double rabbet; the one laps on the door pannel, the other on the quarter pannel, and rises a little above their surface; those pillars are hung with three brass or iron hinges on the fore pillars, and have a box-lock fixed on the opposite pillar, which bolts in the standing pillar; the insides of the door pillars are rabbetted to receive the boardings, which form a case for the glasses, &c.

I. The door top and bottom rails, are tenoned in the door pillars; the top rail, with the addition of an inside piece, forms a top groove for the glass, &c.; the bottom is framed level with the reduced surface of the door pillar, for the pannel to brad against; it is fitted in the large rabbet of the bottom side; and on the bottom is
fixed

fixed a single rabbetted plate, which laps upon, and preserves the pannels.

K. The fore and back seat-rails; the fore seat-rail is tenoned in the standing pillars; the back one is lapped, and screwed on the corner pillar, on a level with each other; on these the boards are nailed which form the seat.

L. The front or middle pillar, lapped and screwed on the middle and top rails, and is grooved the same way as the side of the fore pillars, with partitions for the glasses, &c.

M. The sword-case, so called from its length and convenience for carrying swords or sticks, and, on account of its prominence from the back, is sometimes called a boodge; the ends are made of thick boards, shaped as described, and screwed on the sides of the corner pillars: on the upper part is a rail fixed in the back of the corner pillars, for the boarding to nail against; to which also the octagon-piece is fixed: a rail or batten crosses the two projections, to strengthen the board on the bend.

N. The back-light piece, which is a thick board, out of which the back-light is formed in a square, an octagon, or oval-shape, which is rabbetted for the glass, and, on the edges, for the boards, screwed in the two uppermost rails.

O. The rockers, are two strong boards firmly screwed or nailed to the inner part of the bottom

tom side piece, from which it descends farthest in the middle, and the descent gradually diminishes to both the extremities: on the bottom of these rockers the bottom boards are nailed; their use is to give depth from the seat, without affecting the external appearance of the body.

P. The compass-rails, called hoop-sticks, five or six in number, shaped to the intended form of the roof, and screwed on the top of the side roof-rails; on these the roof-boards are nailed.

Q. The rest-piece for the glasses, on which they fall when let down; they are screwed at the bottom of the grooves, and against which the lining-boards are nailed.

R. The body-loops, which are of iron-work, are fixed on the bottom side-ends with bolts or screws, by which the whole body is supported by the braces.

This is the complete frame-work of a chariot or post-chaise body. The following description is of the body complete, with its pannels and boardings; but as the upper parts are variously finished, it will be necessary to make some observations on the difference.

The upper parts, except the roofs, are generally called upper quarters, that is, side and back quarters. The usual mode of finishing these, is by filling the vacancy with deal boardings, firmly battened

POST-CHAISE BODY.

battened on the infide, and covering the furface with leather, tightly ftrained on, and nailed at the infide edges; over which a moulding goes, and is fewed at the outfide edges, making a welt, or is nailed in a prepared rabbet, and covered alfo with mouldings. Other quarters have the vacancy, the pillars, and rails, covered with a pannel or mahogany board, finely fmoothed on the outfide. The leathered furface is the moft fecure: the pannel furface look   ; but the brads, with which they are confined, and the other nailings of the head-plates, mouldings, &c. occafion them frequently to fplit.

The fword-cafe is prepared in the fame manner as the quarters, either with a leather or mahogany furface.

As the prefent is an improved method of putting in the lower fide pannels in a rounded form, they are thus reprefented. It adds confiderably to the fullnefs of the fide, and exhibits the painting thereon to a much greater advantage: this is done by the door and ftanding pillars being left full on the outfides, and reduced by rounding them towards the bottom.

The infide work, where the glaffes are contained in the front and doors, is only lined or cafed with boardings, and nailed in rabbets on thofe pillars which form the lights or windows: the other infide work is battening, blocking, and glueing

glueing of canvafs, along the edges, and acrofs the grain of the pannels, which glueing very much preferves and ftrengthens them. The blocking is alfo a material affiftance to the ftrength, which is done by a half-fquare, cut acrofs, or angle-ways, cutting it alfo in fhort lengths, and glueing the fquare fides againft the pannel and its framing.

The battens are long, thin pieces of board, placed acrofs the grain of the wood, bradded, or fecured by blocks, or canvafs, in order to ftrengthen or fupport thofe parts to which they are applied.

The infide work, after being thus finifhed, fhould be immediately painted all over, except the feats, and in particular the door and front pannels, before the lining-boards are fixed in, fo as to expofe no timber to the air uncovered with paint, as the air materially affects it, particularly the wide boards, or pannels, as they fwell in wet, and fhrink in dry, feafons: a proper attention, in this particular, is indifpenfably neceffary.

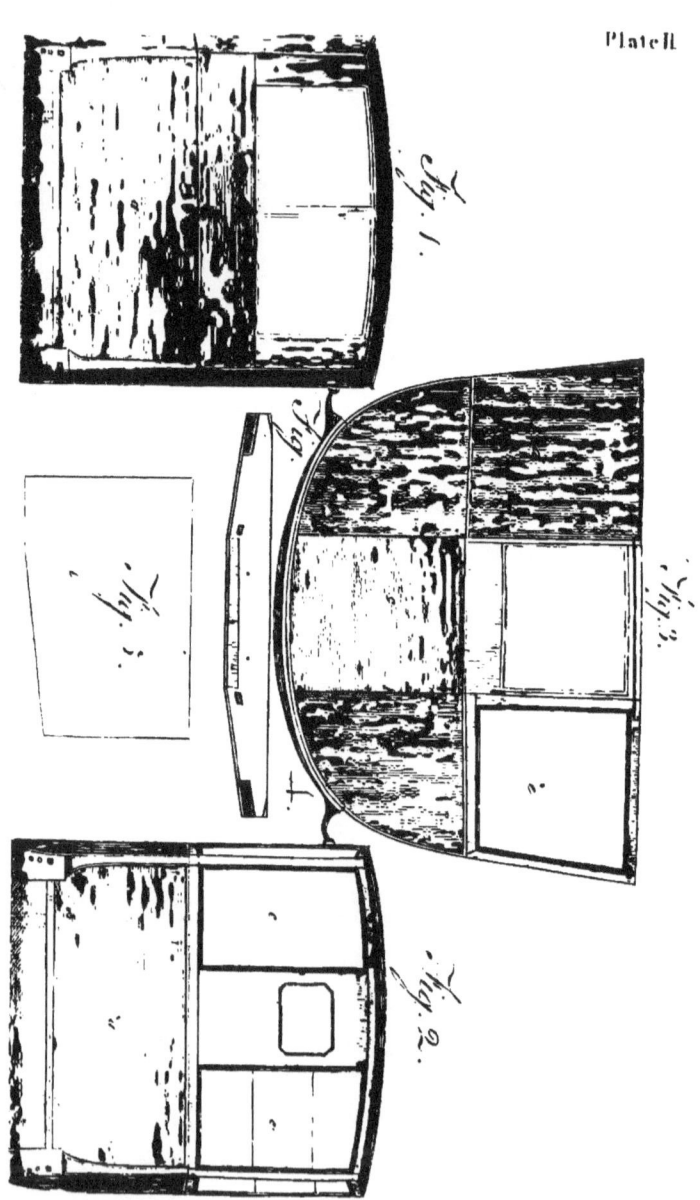

Plate II

SECT. 2.

ON COACH BODIES.

THE accommodation in this body makes it more convenient for large families, being, for the moſt part, capable of holding ſix perſons occaſionally; but as the ſize of the body affects the weight of the whole machine, the proprietor has only to proportion it to the number he wiſhes it to contain; the difference of this from the chariot is only in the length, by the addition of a ſeat ſide; and as every part of the framing bears the ſame name in both, it is unneceſſary to repeat it, but only to obſerve, that the coach has no fore pillar as the chariot has.

PLATE II.

Fig. 1, 2, and 3, ſhew the two ends, or front and back, and the ſide view of a coach or chariot body, with its pannels, or boardings, in the framing, and the uſual method of placing the grain of the wood. The lower pannels are all fixed in grooves; the upper pannels, or boardings, are bradded on the flat ſurface, or in prepared rabbets: the fword-cafe, being an addition depending on choice only, is omitted in this reprefentation, for the purpofe of fhewing the different methods of framing.

Fig. 1, is the fore end, fhewing the method of pannelling the quarters; and

Fig. 2, the hind parts of the body, fhewing the method of boarding the quarters. The one fide of the back is left with the vacancy, on purpofe to fhew the rabbets for the boardings; and the other fide reprefented with the boardings nailed in the rabbets.

Fig. 3, is the fide view, fhewing the upper quarters, the one end boarded, and the other pannelled.

Fig. 4, is the top view of the bottom fide-piece, fhewing the mortices for the ftanding pillars, the rabbet for the door bottom and the end grooves, wherein the corner pillars are fpliced.

Fig. 5, is the half angle of the fide, fhewing one-fourth of the fize within the body, divided at half the extent of the fide and ends.

A. The two end pannels, which are diftinguifhed into back and fore; the grain of the wood they are compofed of is placed length-ways, and is bent by a procefs of heating by fire.

B. The quarter pannels, fixed in the grooves of the bottom fide corner-pillars and elbow rail, and bradded on the ftanding pillars.

C. The

COACH BODIES.

C. The door pannels, fixed in the grooves of the middle door rails, or ſtyles, bradded on the door pillars and door bottom; on which alſo ſmall braſs mouldings are lapped, which ſcrew on to the ſides and bottom of the door.

D. The upper pannels, bradded on to the upper parts of the corner and ſtanding pillars, and to the elbow and top quarter rails, which are rabbetted down to the ſubſtance of the pannel, within about half an inch of the outer edges; the mouldings are afterwards fixed over the joints.

E. The upper quarters, boarded for the purpoſe of being covered with leather: the pillars and rails are rabbetted about half an inch on the inſide edges, for the deal boards to be nailed in.

F. The bottom, which is of ſtrong deal boarding, nailed acroſs to the rockers, and are tongued in each other to exclude the air.

G. The battens, made of wood or thin iron plates, which croſs the boards, and are nailed alſo to the two bottom bars.

H. The roof boardings, which are of thin deals, nailed the long way of the body, and acroſs the hoop-ſticks, to which they are alſo nailed, and prepared ſmooth for the leather.

LANDAU BODIES.

SECT. 3.

LANDAU, OR LANDAULET, BODIES.

THESE kinds of bodies differ nothing in shape from those last mentioned. The landau is the coach, the landaulet the chariot form; so called from the method of opening at the top, which gives the advantage of air and view to the passengers. The top of the whole, from the middle, throws open at pleasure.

These bodies not being assisted by the connected strength of the upper framings, it becomes necessary to make the lower parts of stronger materials, and even to be assisted with strong iron-work, which so increases their weight as to make them objectionable; and this, together with their expence, has almost annihilated the use of them.

The upper parts of these bodies lose much of their appearance, in comparison with those of fixed roofs, as they are covered with loose, oiled leather; that cannot be japanned, and, by being exposed to the weather, contract, and look ill, after being a little time in use; and, now that almost every gentleman is master of the whip, other open carriages are substituted in their place. Many persons, however, are yet partial

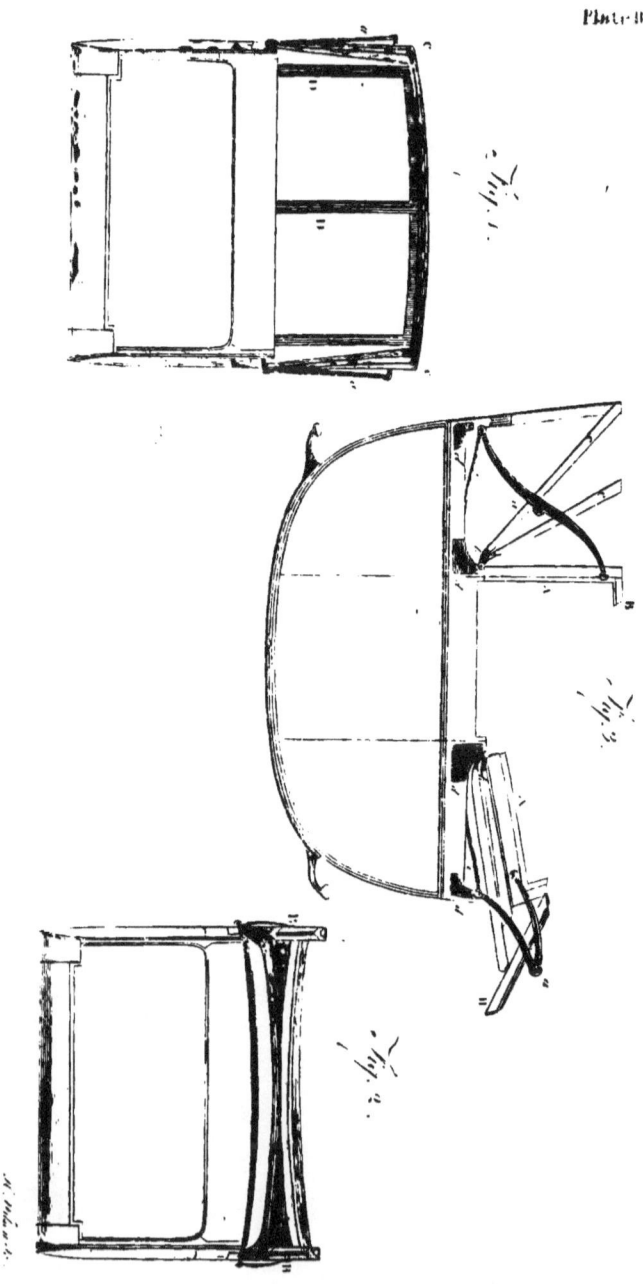

partial to those carriages; for the information of whom, therefore, an exact representation of them is here exhibited. The difference, except in the additional strength of timbers, is only from the middle rails upward, to which height the doors only open; but as mistakes might frequently happen by attempting to open the doors with the glass or shutters up, it is usual to add a spring-bolt on that side of the door which shuts: so that when either the glass or shutter is up, it cannot possibly be opened.

PLATE III.

LANDAU BODY.

Fig. 1, 2, and 3, the front, side, and back views of a landau; the front part shewing the head when fixed, and the back shewing it when down, with the iron-work on, and the usual method of framing these sorts of bodies. The wood-work is described on the plates by capitals, the iron-work by small letters.

A. The standing pillar, which, above the joint, forms the door and standing pillar in one solid piece, and framed in the top rails, to which the fixture for the joint at the top is made fast.

B. The

LANDAU BODY.

B. The door-cafe and door-top rails, imitated in one piece: it is ſtrongly framed to the ſtanding pillar, and divided in two places; between them the joints towards the front are ſecured with a double angle, ſo that, when ſhut, they ſhall not ſhift from each other.

C. The expanding timbers, or hoops, which ſupport the leather, are fixed to the neck-plates, and ſupported by a ſtrong Mancheſter tape, called web: the front and back hoop-ſticks are formed of the front and back top-rails: there are four hoop-ſticks to the middle, or over the door-lights, fixed on the top-rails, two of which unite at the opening joints, on which the faſteners are fixed, to confine the head when up.

D. The front-light pillars, which fall with the reſt of the fore-end, jointed as deſcribed.

a. The iron-joints, which are moſtly plated with ſilver, and fixed on props.

b. The neck-plates, by which the head is fixed up or let down, firmly ſcrewed to the flats, and by which the hoops expand.

c. The ſtay, which ſtrengthens the ſide of the body againſt the ſtrain of the joint.

d. The plates fixed acroſs the joints of the elbow-rails and pillars, to ſtrengthem them.

LANDAULET,

Plate IV

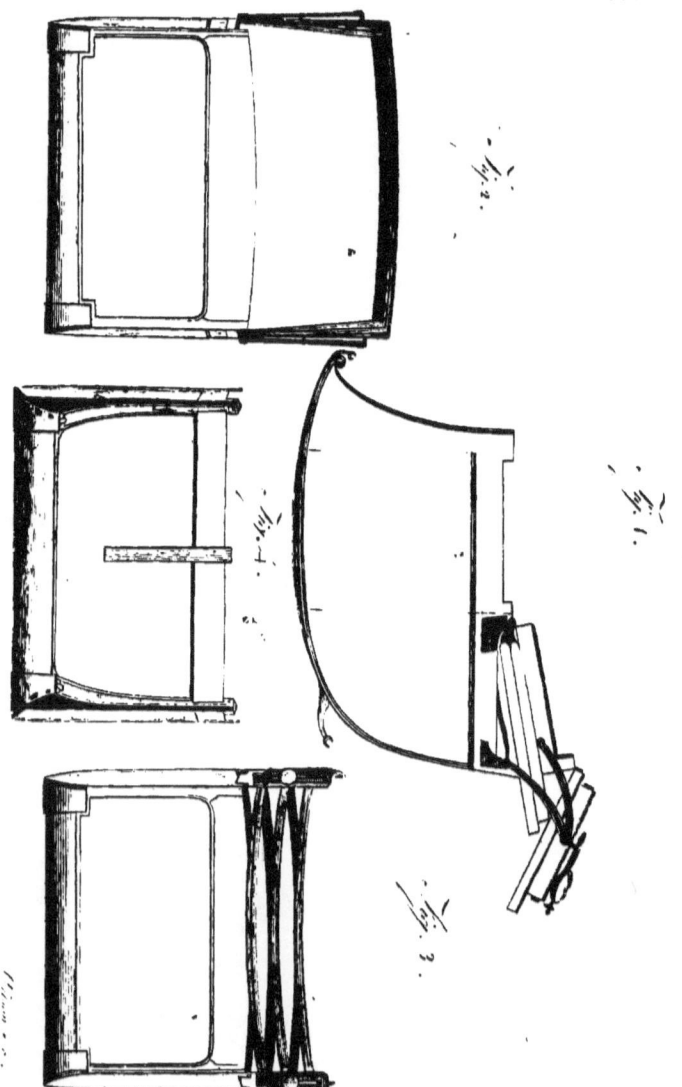

LANDAULET, OR DEMI-LANDAU BODY.

THE difference of this body from that of the landau is very fimple: it has no divifion on the roof, but opens all from the fore part, and throws down behind; whereas the other has two, and opens nearly in the middle of the roof. The ufual method of opening thefe landaulet bodies, is to throw up the roof from the front, and to turn it backwards, throwing the front part forwards; but in this cafe, the lamps muft always be taken off, and laid by.

A better method is to fix the joint on the top, inftead of the middle of the fore pillar, and to turn it up on the infide of the top-cafe rails, which it turns back upon, and falls with the roof, preferving the lamps undifturbed, as reprefented in the plate. The defcription the former chapter explains what further is neceffary to be known in this, which, affifted by the following reprefentation, will prove fufficient information concerning the demi-landau.

PLATE IV.

Four views of the demi-landau, being an addition of a back, which it reprefents when up,
and

and which alſo ſerves for the landau back, the former plate only ſhewing the back when down.

Fig. 1, The ſide view, ſhewing the method by which the roof is turned back, with the lamps on.

Fig. 2, The back, with a fixed top.

Fig. 3, The back, with the top ſtruck down.

Fig. 4, The front, when the top is ſtruck back, with the middle pillars, or partition-piece, turned on the front, which is prevented from touching the pannel by the knuckle of the hinge.

CHAP.

CHAP. II.

PHAETON, CURRICLE, OR CHAISE BODIES.

THESE bodies have a great variety of forms, and are diftinguifhed by their fhape, of which the principal are, the ftep-piece, the tub-bottom, the chair-back, or the half-pannelled bodies: and the *carriage*, with which they are refpectively connected, is called partly by their names, fuch as the ftep-piece phaeton, the tub-bottom chaife, the chair-back curricle, or the half-pannel whifkey carriage, &c.

In thefe open bodies, no one general rule is obferved in building, they being moftly formed to the fancy of the proprietor. Thofe intended for one-horfe carriages are, for the moft part, light; the length of the feat is generally adapted for two perfons only: thofe for two-horfe carriages are generally built of fomewhat ftronger timbers, and are more roomy.—The method of hanging thefe bodies depends much on fancy, or a conception of eafe; and fome bodies are not hung at all, but fixed on the fhafts of their *carriage*, depending

ing entirely for their ease on the springs which are fixed underneath.

Heads to those open bodies are exceedingly convenient in this changeable climate. Some are permanently fixed, and others are made to take off occasionally: but the addition to their weight, and the expence of the heads, frequently render them objectionable, particularly to the very light sort of carriages; in phaetons or curricles, however, drawn by two horses, the objection of weight is done away by the sufficient power of draught.

It would be superfluous here to represent, in the skeleton framing, the great variety of these kinds of bodies. Their different forms are all represented in their finished state in the second volume of this work; and as there is a great similarity in the method of framing them, a representation of two, in which the greatest difference lies, will be sufficient for the whole—the one, a chair-back body, for gig or curricle, which hangs by braces—the other, a simple, half-pannel whiskey, which fixes on the shafts. The former is represented with a head, and the latter with wings only: the head is also represented in the two shapes in which they are used, viz. the square, and the round, or waggon-top form.

The framing, the pannels, and the inside work, are all prepared and fixed to each other in nearly the same manner as the bodies last described, only

only less, and differently shaped: the f   e parts of the framing are   alled by the same name, agreeable to their situations.

SECT. 1.

THE GIG BODY.

THIS kind of body is principally used on a curricle or handsome chaise *carriage*. The hind loops are fixed through the middle back of the corner pillars, by which it hangs: the method of hanging at the fore part varies, according to the fancy of the builder, or the situation of the body. The side pannels may entirely fill the space between the two pillars; but, agreeable to the present mode of building, the side is divided at the standing pillar by a door, or an imitation thereof, preserving the same shape; but, in either case, whether sham or real door, it projects above the surface of the pannel. The size of the body varies according to the purposes for which it is intended, but, in general, measures from two feet ten inches to three feet two inches on the seat.

THE GIG BODY.

PLATE V.

Fig. 1, 2, and 3, The front, back, and side view of a gig body, in the framing only.

A. The bottom side, in which is framed the pillars and brackets.

B. The corner pillars, left with a swell to strengthen and support the loop by which the body hangs, tenoned in the top or elbow rails, and bottom side.

C. The fore pillar, tenoned in the bottom side, and lapped in the elbow rails.

D. The standing pillar, tenoned in the bottom side and elbow rails.

E. The elbow rails, morticed on the corner and standing pillar, and lapped on the fore pillar; on these rails the wings and head are fixed to the side.

F. The back rail, tenoned in the corner pillar, and lapped on the elbow rail, to which it is screwed: on this the pannel brads, and the back of the head is fixed.

G. The front and back seat rails, screwed on the corner pillar, and tenoned in the standing pillar.

H. The bottom bars, tenoned in the bottom side: the pannel brads on the hind one, and the foot-board laps on the fore one, to which it is screwed.

I. The

Plate V.

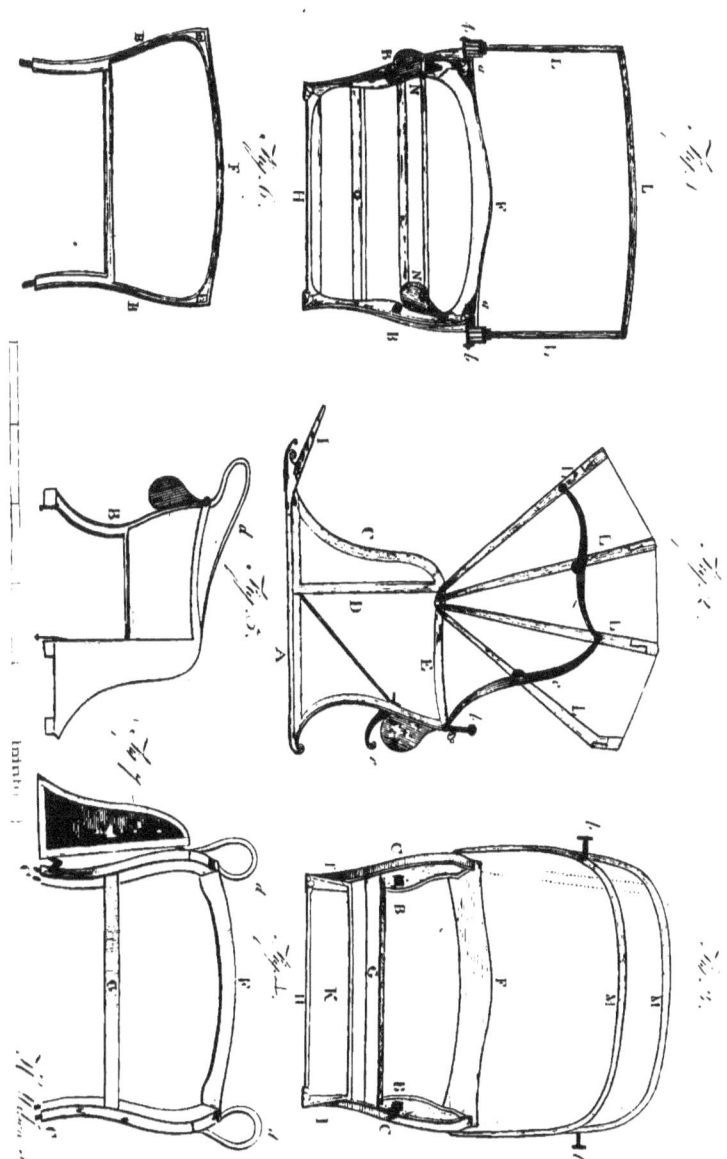

THE GIG BODY.

I. The brackets, tenoned in the ends of the bottom sides: their use is to support the foot-board, in which it is grooved, and screwed from the outside.

K. The foot-board, fixed in the brackets and on the bottom bar.

L. The flats and hoop-sticks, or the timber-work for a square head to support the leather. The side-pieces are called flats, which are separated and fixed by iron-work, and hung on a centre pin, or bolt, to the elbow-rails. The top or roof pieces are called hoop-sticks, which are lapped, nailed, and securely canvassed to the flats, and are placed at proper distances from each other, by means of strong Manchester tape, called girth-webbing, which is nailed to the back rails and to each hoop-stick. On the outsides of the front and third flat, the fixtures or props for the joints are screwed, by means of which the head is put up or let down.

M. The round or waggon-shaped head, the hoop-sticks and flats of which are more curved, are lapped in each other, screwed, and canvassed firmly together: their use and manner of operation is exactly the same as the square heads, of which this, at present, takes the precedence in point of fashion.

N. The sword-case, made the same as the one described in Plate 1.

SECT.

SECT. 2.

HALF-PANNEL OR WHISKEY BODIES.

HALF-pannel bodies are frequently of the same shape as the whole, only the pannels terminate at the seat rail. Lightness in the appearance is the reason for making bodies in this manner, which is seldom made to those of any other shape but that of the tub-bottom. The only difference in these bodies, is their having middle rails framed in the pillars for the pannels to be fixed into, and from the middle rails are open; the bottom-sides, the hind-bar, and pillars, from the middle, are moulded all round, to lighten their appearance.

The common half pannel bodies are those framed on the shafts or timbers of the *carriage*, and have no bottom-sides or foot-board thereto, the foot-boards being fixed to the same timbers or shafts as the body, and are simply framed, as described in Plate 5, Fig. 4, 5, and 6, being the front, back, and side views of a half-pannel whiskey, or chair, with the pannels in the framings, and without a sword-case.

If any of those bodies are made with real doors to open, the fore pillars are not framed to the elbow-rail or bottom-side, but to an additional side-piece,

HALF-PANNEL BODIES.

piece, which hangs by hinges upon the ftanding pillar, having a piece framed acrofs the bottom, with a fmall pannel bradded thereon, the furface of which projects above the other pannel, and is japanned in the fame manner as the quarter or upper parts of a coach. When thefe doors are ufed, the bottom fide, from the ftanding pillar, muft be plated with iron, to afford the neceffary fupport to the fore pillar.

Fig. 7. A real door, hung to the whifkey body, the vacancy on the outfide being covered with pannel or leather. The iron-work is marked with fmall letters, with the intention of fhewing the method of fixing it.

a. The iron frame, on which a head is made, when intended to be taken off occafionally, having the props for the joints and flats thereon.

b. The props for the joints, on which they are fcrewed.

c. The joints, by which the head is fet up or let down at pleafure.

d. The wings, being iron frames, which are covered with ftrong leather when a head is not ufed.

e. The body-loop, which is bolted through the framing, having an iron ftay in the infide, to fupport or preferve the ftrength of the pillar, when the body hangs in this manner.

SECT. 3.

THE VALUE OF BODIES,
IN THEIR NAKED STATE.

TO afcertain the value of bodies and *carriages* feparately, in their unfinifhed ftate, may, by fome, be condemned as an injuftice to the trade, and unprofitable to the public; as it may appear that thofe perfons to whom this fubject is addreffed, would be fufficiently informed, if the value and defcription of the various carriages only, with their additional requifites in their completed ftate, were to be publifhed. This is certainly all that many would defire, but it would not convey a fufficient information to thofe gentlemen who chufe to fpeculate in building their own way; and as impartiality between the public and the trade ought to be regarded, no information fhould be withheld.

The profits to the trade are here proportioned in the fame manner as every other article in the Treatife, and no difadvantage can be complained of, except that of making the public too well acquainted. One material circumftance, in vindication of the neceffity of inferting the prices, is the occafion fome gentlemen have to change the body, or *carriage* part, of that which they immediately

THE VALUE OF BODIES.

mediately occupy, for one of a different fhape, or to fupply the place of an old one; and as the various methods of finifhing every fort are added progreffively in this Treatife, the expence of fuch alterations, any way completed, may be more eafily afcertained.

As the ftuffing on the infide of bodies, and the covering with leather on the outfide, are not to be mentioned hereafter; that matter, with the neceffary iron-work, fuch as loops, locks, hinges, handles, and door-plates, alfo the value of carving them, will be included in the price ftated for each. When thus far finifhed, it will be confidered as a rule to proceed by, and every other article, fuch as lining, painting, and plating, will be added. Whether the quarters and fword-cafe, either of coach or chariot, are covered with leather, or made of mahogany only, it makes no material difference in the expence, but thofe generally prove the beft that are covered with leather.

	£	s.	d.
A chariot body made plain, covered with leather on the roof and quarters, ftuffed or prepared on the infide for the lining; the carving and neceffary iron-work included, as before mentioned	25	0	0
The door-lights contracted on the fides	2	0	0
The body made with round fides, agreeable to the prefent fafhion	1	0	0

A coach

THE VALUE OF BODIES.

	£.	s.	d.
A coach body, plain leathered on the outside, and stuffed on the inside, the carving and iron-work included	30	0	0
Round sides to ditto, extra	2	0	0
A sword-case to either coach or chariot	2	10	0

When carriages are built for hot countries, the bodies are mostly made with lights or windows in the sides and back, to contain blinds and glasses, in the same manner as when they are placed in the door or front, which increases the price of building as follows:

	£.	s.	d.
A pair of side-lights to either	3	10	0
A large back light	2	0	0
Ditto, divided	2	15	0

The landau or demi-landau cannot have any of the extras mentioned in the coach or chariot, except the round sides. Though none of the bodies are represented in the plates with the leather on, its value in this, as in the last, is included with the wood, iron-work, and carving; and the inside is also prepared for the lining, &c. —The extra quantity of workmanship, the increase of iron-work, and difference of leather and putting it on, make the material difference in the price of those bodies from the others. The only difference besides, which is but trifling, is in the trimming or putting in the lining, and which is hereafter particularly noticed

A landau

THE VALUE OF BODIES.   37

	£.	s.	d.
A landau body, with the leather, and iron-work, or the infide ftuffing, &c. thereto	46	0	0
A landaulet, or demi-landau body, as above	40	0	0

The round fides the fame as formerly ftated.

Chaife bodies, being of many different forms, their prices are likewife various; but, owing to their general fimplicity, the difference in their prices is not material. The principal extras, which may be added or omitted to any, are the doors and the fword-cafes. The heads, knee-flaps, and wings, are not included in the prices, but are only reprefented, to fhew the method of making the wood and fixing the iron-work, but are hereafter ftated and fully explained under feparate heads.

The expence of caning, and that of pannelling, the half-formed bodies, is the fame in either. The difference principally lies in the painting or lining, which is afterwards mentioned: the following articles are included in the prices here ftated, viz. all the neceffary iron-work, fuch as loops and ftays; the infides prepared for the lining, and the framings moulded the fame as on the other bodies. No leather is wanting, except to the fword-cafe, and the real or fham doors, which, like the quarters of a coach, may be either leathered or pannelled. This being confidered a rule, the different methods of finifhing may be known, by referring to the separate chapters on lining, painting, plating, heads, wings, knee-flaps, &c.

	£.	s.	d.
A step-piece, or half-shaped body	8	10	0
A gig body, which hangs from the pillars	7	0	0
A common bell, or tub-bottom shaped chaise, which hangs from the bottom corners	6	10	0
A grasshopper or three quarter pannel chaise body	6	6	0
A whiskey or chair body	5	5	0
Doors to open on the sides to either of those bodies	2	0	0
Sham doors to the sides of either	0	15	0
A sword-case, or boodge, to any of them	1	10	0
A drop seat-box to any of the half-pannel bodies, fixed on the seat-rail	0	7	6

CHAP.

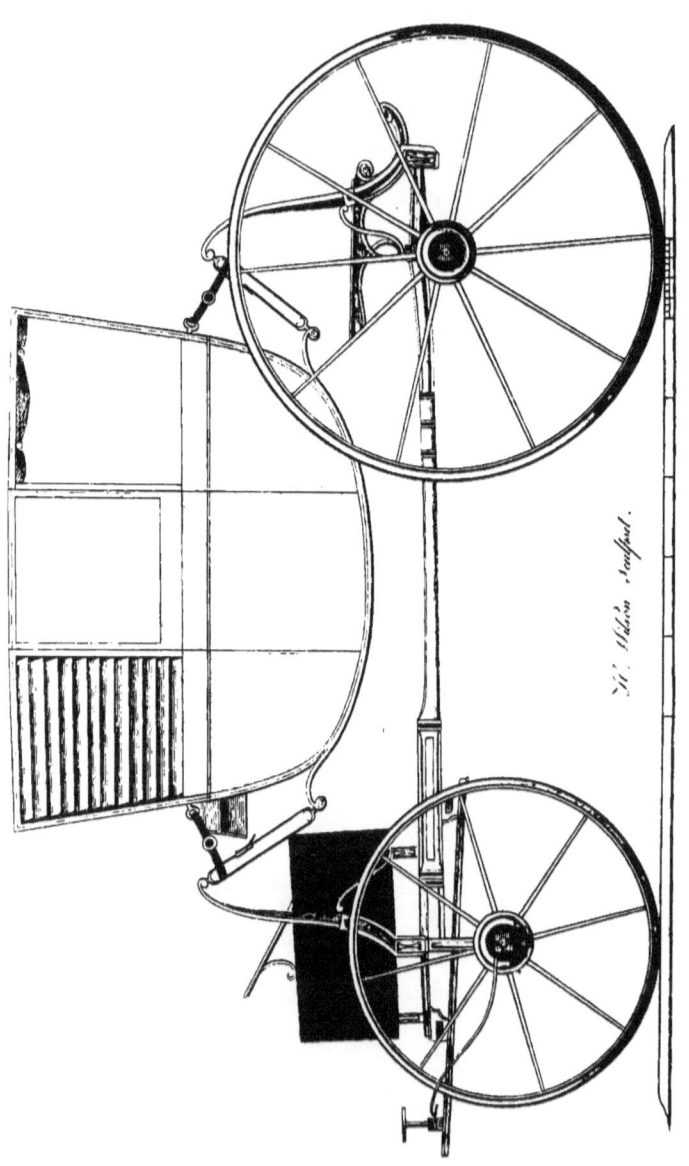

CHAP. III.

FOUR-WHEELED *CARRIAGES.*

THOUGH, as before obferved, by the term *Carriage* is generally underftood a carriage complete, yet its meaning is frequently confined to the under part only, on which the body is placed. It is the *carriage* which bears the ftrefs of the whole machine, and much depends on its fufficiency. It fhould be well proportioned in its ftrength, according to the weight it is meant to fupport, always allowing rather an over proportion, than running the rifk of accidents. A proper application of the iron-work, to fupport the preffure, is a material thing to be attended to; and great care fhould be taken that no flaws be permitted to pafs. The timbers, which are of afh, fhould be of young trees of the ftrongeft kind, free from all kinds of knots, and perfectly feafoned before ufed; and, as many parts of the framing are obliged to be curved, it is beft to felect fuch timbers as are grown to the fhape.

FOUR - WHEELED *CARRIAGES*.

The workmanship of a *carriage* must be particularly firm, and not partially strained in any part, as it is to bear much racking in its use. The timbers throughout are lightened or reduced, for the sake of external appearance, assisted also with moulding edges, and carving in some small degree, which greatly helps to ornament the whole.

All four-wheeled *carriages* are divided into two parts—the upper and under *carriage*. The upper is the main one, on which the body is hung; the under *carriage* is the conductor, and turns by means of a lever, called a pole, acting on a centre pin, called a perch-bolt. The hind wheels are placed on the upper part; the fore wheels on the under.

There are two sorts of four-wheeled *carriages* —the perch and crane-neck, in which there is a material difference in the building and properties: but this does not affect the bodies, as they will hang equally on either. The perch *carriage* is of the most simple construction, and considerably lighter than the crane-neck; and as the width of the streets in this metropolis gives every advantage to their use in turning, they are the most general. The crane-neck *carriage* has much the superiority for convenience and elegance, and every grand or state equipage is this way built; but the weight of the cranes, and the additional

additional ftrength of materials neceffary for their fupport, make them confiderably heavier than the others; but their eafe and fafety in turning in narrow, confined places, and alfo their ftrength, render them indifpenfably neceffary for foreign countries.

The track in which the wheels of every *carriage* are to run, is generally the fame, except when intended for particular roads, where waggons and other heavy carriages are principally ufed; they leave very deep ruts, in which light carriages muft likewife go.

All four-wheeled carriages fhould have the hind and fore wheels regulated to roll in the fame track; the ordinary width of the wheels is four feet eight or ten inches; that of waggons or carts generally meafure five feet two inches; to which chaife wheels, being principally intended for the country, are adapted. It is immaterial to what width wheels are fet, if ufed for running upon ftones; but on marfhy roads, if their exactnefs is not attended to, the draught is confiderably increafed. The different heights of hind and fore wheels make alfo a difference in the length of their axletrees, agreeable to the proportion they bear to one another : the fore wheel has the longeft axletree, by one or two inches between the fhoulders.

The

The length of the *carriage* is regulated by the size or length of the body it is intended to carry, but always takes its measure from the two centres of the hind and fore axletrees. In general, a perch *carriage* measures nine feet two inches for a chariot, and nine feet eight inches for a coach: a crane-neck *carriage*, on account of the bow for the wheels to pass under, measures, for a chariot, nine feet six inches—for a coach, ten feet.

In phaetons, the variety being so great, there is no rule to go by, as it depends on the situation the body is placed in, and whether intended for one or two horses; but their construction is similar to the rest. Many persons are of opinion, that by contracting the length of the *carriage*, a material difference is made in the draught; but the advantage thereby gained is trifling in comparison with the ease and elegance of a carriage of a proper length: besides, the resemblance they have to common hackney carriages, ought to be a sufficient objection to their use.

The forms of building four-wheeled *carriages* (except in the difference of perch and crane neck) are nearly the same in all. The timbers are united to the perch in one general way; as are also the timbers to the cranes; so that one representation of each *carriage*, which is of a chariot proportion, by shewing the views, and describing their several parts, will sufficiently explain

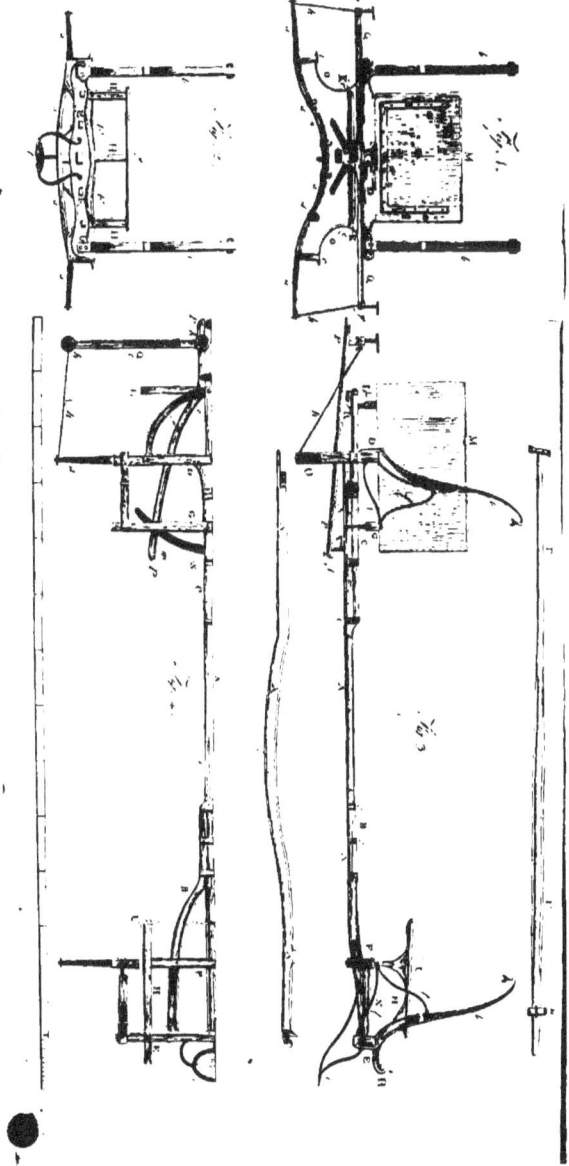

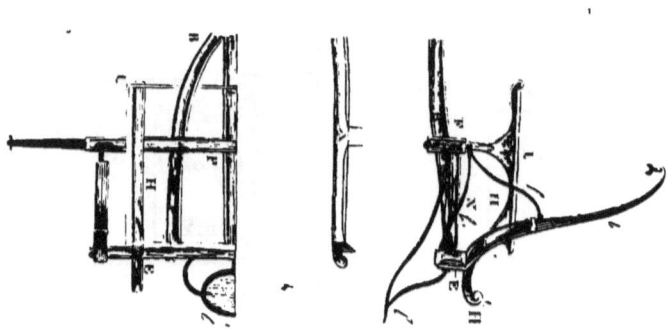

plain the whole: their iron-work is alfo defcribed, for the better information in that material article.

SECT. 1.

DESCRIPTION OF PERCH *CARRIAGES*.

PLATE VI.

Fig. 1, 2, 3, and 4, are the front, the back, the fide, and top view of a perch carriage, without a coach-box. The length defcribed is that of a chariot *carriage*, but the reprefentation will anfwer for either coach or phaeton: the length of the perch, and the ftrength of materials, make the only difference.

Fig. 1, is the front, fhewing the under *carriage* united with the upper, the proper length and depth of the fore tranfom and fore axletree bed, and in what manner the futchels are fixed in the bed, and how the fplinter-bar is placed on the futchels with the wheel-irons on, fhewing the axis, and the manner it is confined in the bed, and the length of the arms on which the wheel goes, the fore tranfom has the boot and fprings fixed thereon, fhewing the proper fituation of the fprings, and how faftened.

Fig.

Fig. 3, is the fide view, principally fhewing the perch, and how connected with the other timbers at the hind and fore ends (the ends of the timber acrofs the perch is only feen), the fprings and ftays in their proper fituation, and how the fhort blocks are placed on the hind, and the boot on the fore end, when ufed.

Fig. 4, is the half-top view, fhewing in what manner the timbers are framed acrofs the perch, and how otherwife confined; the hind foot-board and boot are lightly reprefented, fo as not to prevent the fight of the under framings.

A. The perch, which is the main timber of the *carriage,* by extending through the hind and fore fpring tranfom or bars. By it the principal part of the upper *carriage* is fupported. The hind part is fupported and united to it by means of hooping two extending timbers, called wings, on the fide. The fore end is fixed or united to the perch by means of a ftrong piece hooped at the top, and framed through the fore tranfom, called a hooping-piece: but fome *carriages* have a horizontal wheel in the front, the fame as the crane-neck *carriages*; and thefe have no hooping piece to the perch, but are fecured by means of fide-plates. Thofe on the general principle have, at the bottom in front, a flat piece, left extended, called a tongue, which goes through a large mortice in the fore axletree bed, and through which

the

the perch-bolt paffes: its ufe is to keep the fore axletree bed fteady in its place.

Sometimes the perch is made of a bent form, called a compafs perch, for the purpofe of admitting the body to hang low, or to form a more agreeable line to the fhape thereof: thofe perches are of a very ancient form, but are now revived with confiderable improvement from their original fhape, and are become the prevailing fafhion. In order to give a proper defcription of them, a compafs perch is introduced between the two views, to fhew their prefent fhape: when the *carriage* is intended for a whole or horizontal wheel, the perch has no hooping-piece, but is bolted by the plates at each end to the infide of the tranfoms.

Plating with iron the fides of perches is a great improvement, and is now moft generally done, and always muft be, to thofe compafs perches, if required to be light in their appearance, as the fize of the timber is fo much reduced by cutting them to this fhape.

To the ftraight or compafs perch, iron plating on the fides is a great addition, as it will admit the timbers to be fo much reduced, that a fufficient ftrength is preferved, though but half the ufual fize; the plates, as fixed edge-ways to the fides of the perch, will fupport ten times more weight than if flat-ways on the bottom, which is

the

the method of plating a perch in the plain or common way; and many of thofe carriages which are made up for fale have even the bottom plate omitted; but the certain confequence of this fuperficial method is, the finking or fettling of the perch, whereby the *carriage* is contracted quite out of its form, to the great injury of it, both for ufe and appearance, and there is no remedy but by a new one.

B. The hind hooping-wings, fo called from their extended form, are the principal fupport of the hind framings, being hooped on the fides of the perch, and extend to the hind fpring tranfom, through which they are framed: they alfo help to fupport the axletree bed, which is bolted thereon.

C. The fore hooping-piece, is a large timber hooped on the top of the perch, and which unites the fore end to it, being ftrongly framed through the fore tranfom or fpring-bar; extending to the out circumference of the horizontal half-wheel, which it alfo helps to fupport, when there are no fore wings; on it the budget-bar refts, and is fixed thereto.

D. The fore tranfom, or fore fpring-bar, is the moft effential part of the crofs framings. It is a ftrong timber fixed to the perch by means of a hooping-piece, or otherwife receives a tenon of the perch, if a hooping-piece is not ufed, which perch is also strengthened by means of plates bolted to their sides and to the transom. The fore or under *carriage* is confined hereto by means of a large, round, iron pin, called the perch-bolt, passing through its centre: on the bottom is a thick, flat plate, made flush to the edges, called a transom-plate: on the ends the springs are fixed; and on the top the boot, or the block that supports it, is placed: between the springs and the boot, the usual coach-box also is fixed.

E. The hind transom, or hind spring-bar, something similar in its use with the fore transom, but not required to be of such strength. In it the perch, and the timbers which run parallel with it, are framed; and on the ends the hind springs are fixed, the blocks or pump-handles are placed on the top, and the footman's step bolted on the outside.

F. The hind axletree-bed, a strong timber which receives the axletree. It is fixed by being bolted to the perch, and the wings on which it is lapped or sunk. In this, and in the spring bed, are two small timbers tenoned, called nunters: one of the bearings of the blocks rests on this bed, as also do the spring-stays. The bottom is grooved to receive the axletree, which is called bedding for the axletree, but is mostly bedded at the ends only, excepting when the axletree lies above the perch, or when the perch is framed
through

through the bed, in which cafe the axletree is bedded all the length of the timber. At the two ends of this timber are left projections, called cuttoos, which cover the top or back end of the wheels, to fhelter the axletree-arms from the dirt, which would otherwife get in behind the wheels, and clog them.

G. The budget-bar, frequently called a horn-bar, from the original fhape thereof, but it is now only a ftraight timber, on which refts the boot or budgets, or the blocks that fupport them. It has only a bearing in the middle on the perch: on it, at the ends, which are fometimes focketted, the fore fpring-ftays reft, for which ufe it is principally calculated, affifted materially in its ftrength by an iron ftay, which fixes to the bottom of the perch and at each end of this bar.

H. The hind blocks, which, when further extended than what is here reprefented, are called pump-handles: they are frequently called raifers; their ufe is only to heighten the platform from the hind framings, that the appearance may be light, and that the footman may be fufficiently raifed according to the height of the body: they are bolted on to the axletree bed and fpring-bar; and, to leffen their too heavy appearance, are often neatly ornamented with carving.

I. The foot-board, or platform, on which the trunk, the cufhion, or the fervant ftands, is a

flat

PERCH *CARRIAGES.* 47

flat, thick, elm board, bolted on with the blocks, to which it is also screwed.

K. The wheel-piece, is a casing on the horizontal half-wheel plate, and is of no other use than to ornament the iron, which it is placed on, being screwed from the bottom of the plate, and fixed a little way in the transom.

L. The fore block, an ornament at the front part, fixed on the top end of the fore hoopingpiece, and supports the boot or budget in the middle of the front, to which it is bolted: this block is mostly united to the side-blocks, or raisers, of the boot.

M. The boot, a large, square box, framed and boarded, and is sometimes made of strong elm boards, nailed and screwed together, having a door in the front, which should be framed and boarded, and confined by a bolt and thumb-nut. The surface of this boot should always be covered with a russet, or japanning leather: it is bolted across the transom, the boot-bar, and boot-block; and is sometimes raised on side-blocks to lighten the appearance of the fore end.

N. The nunters, are two short pieces of timber fixed under the block, and tenoned in the axletree-bed and spring-bar, to assist their strength, and keep them more securely together.

O. P. Q. and *R.* The fore or under *carriage,* united to the upper *carriage* by the perch-bolt.

Vol. I. F *O.* The

O. The fore axletree-bed, a large, strong piece of timber, in which the fore axletree is bedded: on this the upper *carriage* rests; it has a large mortice near the top, in which the perch-tongue is placed. In this timber the futchels are fixed: it has also cuttoos on the ends the same as the hind bed has.

P. The futchels, are two light timbers, fixed through the fore axletree-bed, nearly of the shape of the hind hooping-wings; contracted in the front, to receive the pole, which part of the futchels is called the chaps; but widens towards the hind end, on the top of which the sway-bar is placed; on the fore ends, and across the chaps the splinter-bar is fixed. They are framed in a slant direction, to give a proper height to the pole; but when a whole wheel is in the front, then the futchels are framed in a horizontal direction, and are made to rise obliquely from the front of the horizontal wheel, otherwise the pole must be made compassed, to raise it to a proper height for the horses.

Q. The splinter-bar, a long timber to which the horses are fastened, and is fixed on with roller-bolts near the fore end of the futchels, from which it is a little raised, to admit the pole being placed in the chaps: on the ends are sockets with eyes, in which the wheel-irons are placed, and also

PERCH *CARRIAGES*. 51

from thence to the axletree arms, contracting the splinter bar tightly back, to oppose the tugging by draught, which is taken from the roller-bolts, at the ends and middle.

R. The front felly-piece, is a small part of the same circle as the upper wheel-plate, made to fill the space between it and the futchels, to which it is bolted. Its use is to make a firm bearing for the upper *carriage* to work on; so that, in whatever direction the fore *carriage* may be, a steadiness is always preserved.

S. The sway-bar, is a timber forming part of a circle made for a bearing against the perch, as far as the locking of the fore wheels makes it necessary. Its use is to preserve a steady action of the fore *carriage*: it is bolted on the back ends of the futchels, usually plated on the top ends with iron: the middle is lined with hard leather, to prevent a noise in use.

T. The pole, a long timber which occasionally is placed in the futchel-chaps, being nicely fitted therein, and is confined by two plates, the one bolted at the bottom in front, and the other at the top, at the back end of the chaps: it is also secured by a wooden pin, called a gib, which is placed across the futchels, and in a staple which is in the pole: an iron pin also goes through the futchels and the pole at the fore end;

on each fide of the pole the horfes are placed, and ſtrapped to a loop at the fore end, called a pole-ring: its uſe is to conduct the fore *carriage*, and may properly be called a *carriage* lever.

U. The pole-gib, is a ſmall piece of wood, made flat at the bottom, and is rounded at the top, to fit the ſtaple in the pole, which it keeps from riſing up at the fore end, nailed on by a loofe ſtrap to the futchels, and kept in its place by another ſtrap nailed on the oppoſite fide, which is hitched on a brafs or plated button.

Although the iron-work and its properties are feparately defcribed in the Plate, yet the explanation will be more clear by pointing out here their fituations, which is done in ſmall letters placed againſt the different parts, which are named as follow:

 a. The hind and fore axletrees.
 b. The hind and fore fprings.
 c. The perch and axle-hoops.
 d. The axletree-clips.
 e. The tranfom and wheel plates.
 f. The fpring-ſtays.
 g. The fplinter-bar fockets.
 h. The wheel-irons.
 i. The fide perch-plates.
 k. The fplinter-bar rolls.
 l. The footman's ſtep.

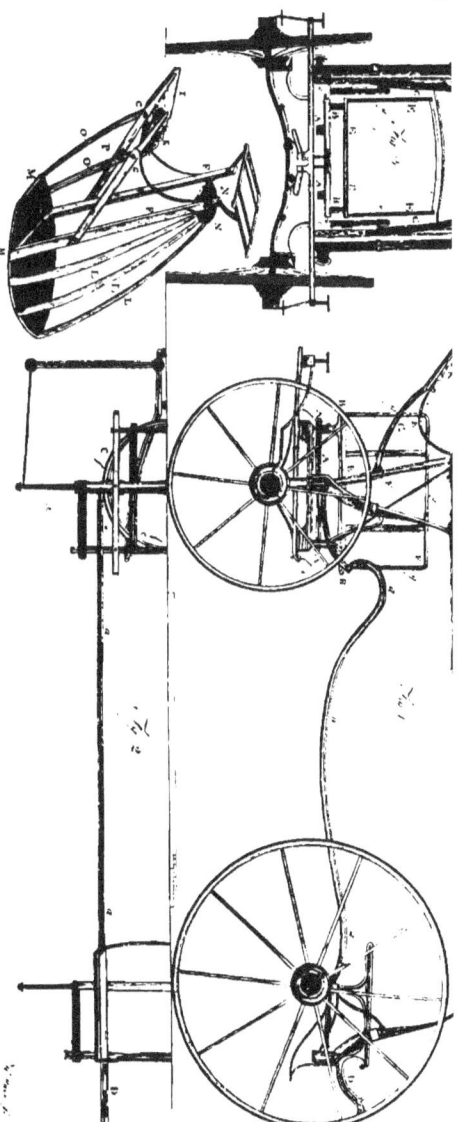

Plate

m. The fway-bar plates.
n. The budget-plate.

SECT. 2.

CRANE-NECK *CARRIAGES*.

Fig. 1, 2, and 3, reprefent a chariot crane-neck *carriage*, in the fide, the top, and fore end views, with the coach-box, and a platform, or luggage-boot, in their proper fituations. The wheels are added to this *carriage*, fhewing their proper height and diftance from each other, commonly called the track; alfo the circumference which the fore wheels take in turning, by which the bows of the cranes are regulated in their diftance, and in their height, by the height of the wheels.

The timbers of this *carriage* are of the fame defcription of the laft, excepting the perch and hooping-timbers, which, in this fort of *carriage*, are not ufed. The hind and fore ends are fixed to the cranes, which makes the bearings more fteady than thofe of a perch *carriage*. The addition of wood-work to this *carriage*, may be added to the laft defcribed, and is as follows:

A. The crofs framings, called wings, or fore nunters, which are framed through the fore tranfom, and fupport, at the two ends, the horn-bar and fore-bars.

B. The fide-blocks, bearing on the tranfom, the horn, and fore bars, to which they are confined by bolting.

C. A whole wheel-front, which is neceffary for all crane-neck *carriages*, for the purpofe of preferving a fteady bearing to the fore *carriage* while turning round. This fort of fore end is alfo frequently ufed to the perch *carriage*, and is a great improvement thereto.

D. The hind blocks, the fame as *H* laft defcribed, only are made longer behind, in order to affift the fervant in mounting, and are called pump-handles.

E. The platform, or luggage-boot, made only as a platform, being a thick, elm board, with ledges fcrewed round to ftrengthen it, and to receive the irons which form the fhape for the fides, and are bolted on the bottom, having two pieces fixed upright to fupport the irons in the middle, having alfo two flats, or hoop-fticks, fixed acrofs, which loop in ftaples fixed in thofe upright pieces, to fupport the cover in the middle.

The coach-boxes, which are of two general forts, fuch as the Standard and Salifbury, are fhewn apart, and defcribed at *I, K, L, M, N, O, P*, which directs the method of framing them :—

the

CRANE-NECK CARRIAGES.

the Salifbury is reprefented in perfpective; the other in two views with the *carriage*.

F. The fore ftandards; the main pillars of the coach-box, which fupport the feat, are fixed on the fore tranfom by plates, and are alfo fupported by a ftay bolted to the horn-bar.

G. The ftays, framed in the ftandards, and curved upwards to receive the foot-board, which is fixed thereon, and ftrengthened by an iron compaffed ftay.

H. The box-bars, framed in the ftandards to keep them fteady at top.

I. The fore foot-board, for the coachman to place his feet againft, having his purchafe affifted by a ledge fcrewed thereon. The foot-board is bolted on the ftays, which are confined and ftrengthened by it.

K. The brackets, or ledges, two pieces of wood, which are carved, and fixed on the foot-board fides for ornament only.

L. The flats, or ribs, firmly fcrewed or nailed in the bottom and top, which form the boot behind, and fupport the leather that is ftrained round them.

M. The bottom, made of two ftrong elm boards placed acrofs each other, and to which the other timbers are fixed, affifted alfo with iron-work.

N. A ftrong

N. A strong board fixed on the top bar, projecting back, for the ribs to be fixed into.

O The two upright stays, which form the boot in front, and support the other stays by being bolted thereto.

P. The front, which is always boarded over the vacancy, for the leather to be placed upon.

The iron-work to this *carriage*, which is different from the last, is only here to be described, and that also in small letters.

a. The cranes, with single bows, and a little formed on the hind sweep.

b. The back-stays, which support the coach-box.

c. The compass-irons, which support the foot-board and stays.

d. The seat-irons, with a stay to each, on which the cradle for the seat is to be fixed.

e. The standard-plates, with which the coach-box is fixed to the transom, by clipping on it between the boot and springs, and is secured by two bolts to each.

f. The whole or horizontal wheel-plate, fixed to the bottom of the fore transom and horn bar, for the fore *carriage* to lock steady by.

g. The luggage boot-irons, with which the boot is made or formed on the side, having the vacancy covered with leather.

Those

Those two *carriages* are represented and described principally as a post-chaise or chariot; but both representations and descriptions will answer for coaches and phaetons, either perched or crane-necked; the difference lies only in the length, and not in the form; which difference may be known from the further descriptions given of carriages in the finished state: the boots, the coach-boxes, and the raised hind and fore ends, are only represented here, for information how they are placed when intended for coach or chariot.

CHAP.

CHAP. IV.

TWO-WHEELED *CARRIAGES.*

THOSE *carriages* have the advantage of all others for simplicity and lightness; but in this sort of carriage there is more risk than in those that are four-wheeled, particularly if the horse is not tractable and sure-footed. That which makes the variety of this sort of *carriage*, is the method of placing the bodies, whether hung from springs or fixed on the *carriage*, which is decided principally by the fancy of the occupier: the generality fall under the description of curricles, gigs, whiskies, or chairs; but that wherein the principal difference lies, is the curricle, being formed for two horses abreast, which at present is the most fashionable carriage in use; the gig from the whiskey also differs materially, the whiskey being constructed on the most simple plan, with the body united to the *carriage*, while the gig exhibits a greater portion of fancy, having the bodies hung in various directions; it is by the form of the *carriage*, and the method of placing the

the body, that they are named; as gig, curricle, &c.

Thofe open carriages are generally intended for the country, and are made longer on the axletree than in other carriages intended for town ufe only, in order that the wheels may fall or go in the waggon tracks.

The ftrength of the *carriage* in this, as in all others, is to be regulated by the fize of the body which it is meant to fupport, as alfo the places in which it is to be ufed; as in rough roads an addition of ftrength is required in building. The timbers are ufually of afh; but a preferable method of building, is to make the fhafts of a foreign timber, of the Weft-India growth, called lance-wood, which is of fufficient ftrength, even when reduced to half the fize of afh, and is fo remarkably elaftic as to give great eafe to the rider, and always preferves the fhape; whereas the afh fhafts are obliged to be made clumfy, and foon fettle by the weight, and, befides, require to be affifted in their ftrength with iron plates at the bottom, which cannot at all be applied to the lance-wood fhafts, on account of their elafticity. The draught is much preferable when taken from a fplinter-bar, which yields to the motion and pull of the horfe; and the nearer to the axle the fixtures, ufed to draw by, are placed, fo as not to be very low from the purchafe,

TWO-WHEELED *CARRIAGES*.

chafe, the lighter is the draught. The *carriage* should be so made, that the axletree may be placed nearly on an equilibrium; so that, when the paffengers are in the body, the weight may not exceed 30lb. on the back of the horfe; obferving alfo to have room at the ftep, fo as not to be obftructed by the wheel on entering the carriage.

The variety of thofe two-wheeled *carriages* can be underftood better by the reprefentation given on the plate than by defcription, as they are all fimilar in their conftruction, though very different in their ufe: but, compared to other forts of *carriages*, they are very fimple. The materials of which they are compofed are but few, and their purpofes nearly the fame in each; fo that one defcription, affifted with the general reprefentation in the plate, will furnifh every information neceffary on that fubject.

PLATE VII.

Fig. 1, 2, 3, 4, 5, and 6, The fide and top views of a curricle, gig, and whifkey *carriage*, being the three moft generally in ufe.

Fig. 1 and 2, The fide and half-top reprefentation of a curricle *carriage*, framed wide and long,

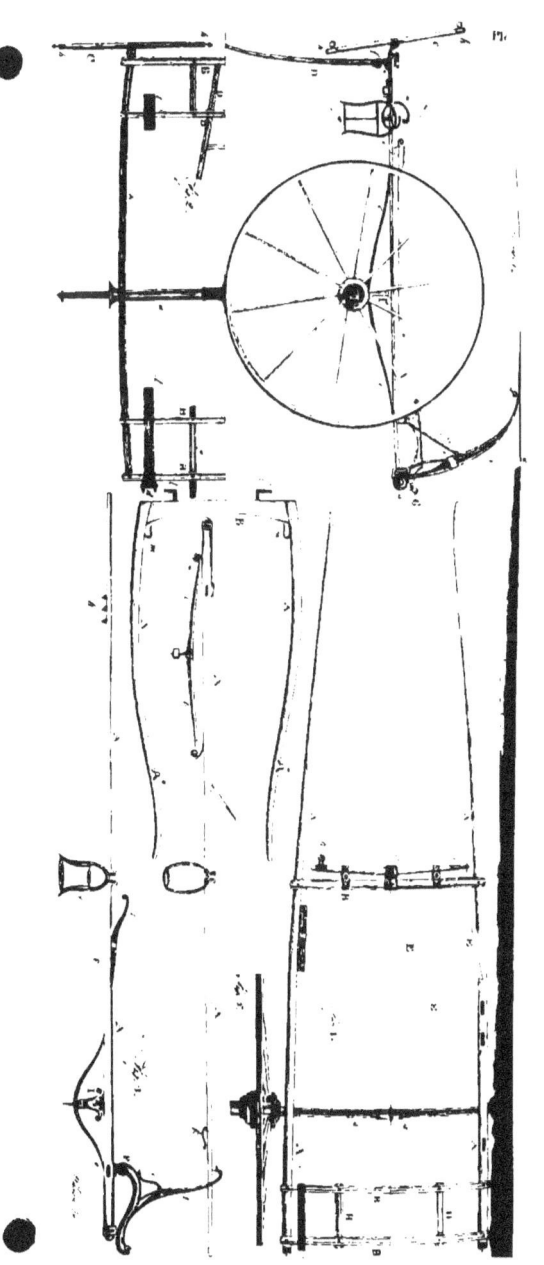

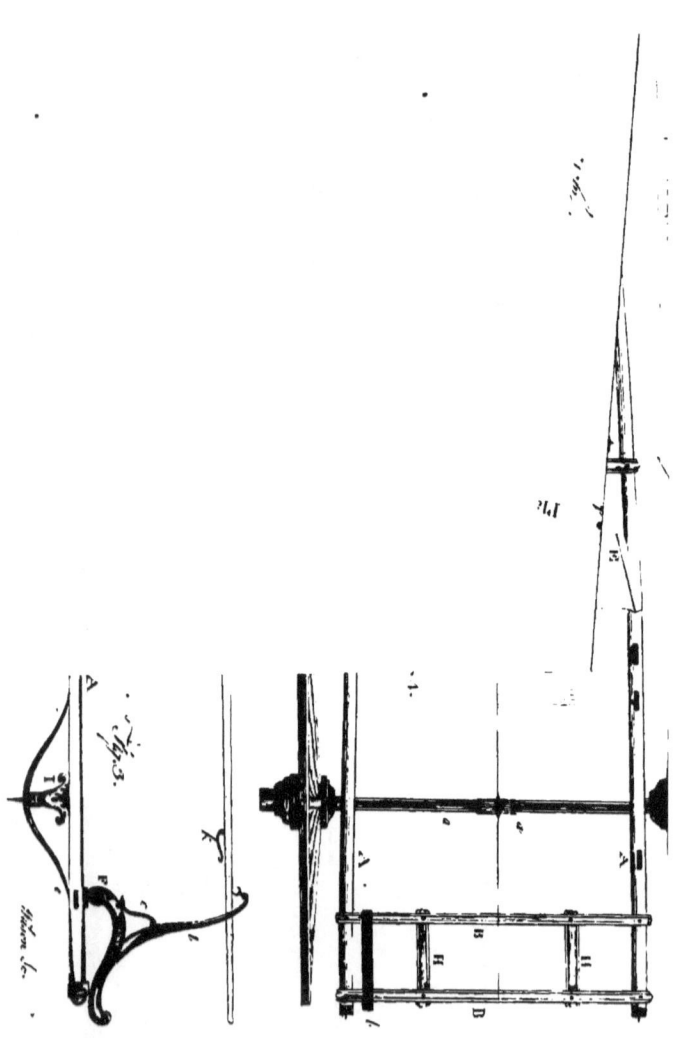

TWO-WHEELED CARRIAGES.

long, for the purpose of admitting the body to hang between, which is the present mode of building.

Fig. 3 and 4, A gig *carriage*, in the same views as the curricle, with the wheels added, shewing their distance apart. The body in this representation is supposed to hang above the shafts; therefore the *carriage* is not so long or wide between the framings, which is always prepared according to the method or fancy of hanging the bodies. Those *carriages* are made to either pattern, and for either use, excepting the shafts to the gig, and the additional framing at the fore part of the curricle.

Fig. 5 and 6, The same views of a whiskey or chaise *carriage*, for the building of which there is but one rule, the body being framed or fixed on the shafts, having the footboard and bottom also secured thereto.

Fig. 7, The shafts, used to a one-horse four-wheeled carriage, which hang loosely on the horse, answering the purpose of a pole to turn or lock the *carriage* by.

A. The shafts, which are the side framings and principal part of the *carriage*, by which it is supported by the horse: they are regulated to a general width at the point, measuring two feet three inches across; the length from the bar of
draught

draught is fix feet fix inches, and the height in proportion to that of the horfe intended; but are, in general, made to thofe of a middle fize, or 15 hands: thofe to a curricle, are only properly called fhafts, that are applied when one horfe is ufed to that fort of *carriage;* the others ought only to be called fide-framings; in thofe, as alfo in the proper fhafts, the crofs-bars are framed, and are tenoned, morticed, or lapped, as the builder's judgment may direct; affifting alfo, where ftrength is required, by plates, uniting the bars with the fhafts, particularly in the curricle at the fore ends, which cannot be made too fafe.

B. The crofs-framings, called hind or fore bars: thofe on which the fprings are fixed, are called fpring-bars; the front bar to a single-horfe *carriage* is what the draught is moftly taken from, by means of a fplinter hung thereto; the additional fore-bars to a curricle are to affift the ftrength, and form a bearing for the pole, which by a clofe leather brace are fixed in fockets at their bottom.

C. The fplinters, or fplinter-bars, hung on the fore-bar to chairs, or in loops to curricles, having iron-work at the ends called fockets, for the traces to be faftened to.

D. The ladder-prop for the curricle, which it fupports while ftanding, or when the horfes are

putting

putting to: it is fixed on the fore-bar, with jointed iron-work, which, when the horſes are put to, admits it to be thrown back to the back-bar, where it is ſecured by means of a ſpring catch, or a ſtrap and buckle.

E. The brackets, the foot-board, and the bottom of a whiſkey, which are fixed on the ſhafts, and conſtitute a part of the carriage.

F. The hind and fore blocks, on which the ſprings are placed, are chiefly uſed as an ornament to this ſort, as well as to phaeton carriages.

G. Small blocks, for ſupporting a platform, which they raiſe above the bars, and which lighten its appearance, and may be uſed or omitted at pleaſure.

H. The croſs-framings, called nunters, which ſerve to ſtrengthen and fill the ſpace between the bars.

I. The raiſers, which ſupport the ſhafts from the axletree; ſometimes are only turned, and ſometimes carved, to ornament the carriage.

a. The axletree.
b. The ſprings.
c. The ſpring-ſtay.
d. The ſpring-jacks.
e. The main or bottom ſtays, terminating in loops at the curricle's fore-end, and at the fore-bar in a chaiſe.

f. The

f. The ladder-joints.
g. The steps, double and single.
h. The splinter-sockets.
i. The curricle-sockets for shafts.
k. The tug-plates or flops.
l. The hooks by which these shafts hang on the splinter-bar.
m. The hooks the traces are fixed to.
n. The breeching-staples.

PRICE OF CARRIAGES.

ON account of the great variety in the form and fize of *carriages*, it would be difficult to affix the exact value of every different defcription of them; but, to take them in the moft general way they are built, and omitting fome particulars to be by themfelves treated of, they may be reduced to a rule, regulating them to five claffes, viz. the coach, the chariot, the large, the middle and fmall-fized phaetons. The two former only have coach-boxes; the reft generally have boots, and alfo raifed fore and hind ends, properly called platforms.—Therefore, to reduce the price of *carriages* to any certain rule, thofe articles muft all be excepted; and a reference to the defcriptions and prices of them, which are afterwards ftated, will enable the proprietor to know how to add any of thofe requifites, and be a competent judge of the value and form of whatever kind of *carriage* his fancy may lead him to make choice of.

Coach and chariot *carriages* are built exactly fimilar to each other; the only difference is the fuperior ftrength of the materials.

Phaetons have a great fimilarity to them; but the fituation of the fprings, which are placed in various directions for the body to hang from, makes the appearance the only material difference from other *carriages*: so that, by excepting the blocks and budgets, they will be reduced to the same principle as the others.

The workmanship is nearly the same in value to all *carriages* on the plain system. The materials are somewhat reduced in their value for the lesser *carriage*, and bear the reduction of one-tenth from each other. Their value, when thus far executed, is what is reckoned the first charge or rule to follow; the wheels, the boots, the coach-boxes, the raised hind or fore ends, the blocks for the springs, and also the painting, are added afterwards; so that, in whatever manner they are completed, their value may be ascertained.

The additions to two-wheeled *carriages* are very few above what are represented in the plate: the platform and budgets behind the dashing-leather, and the odds of double steps before, are the principal of the additions, and which are particularly mentioned hereafter.

THE

THE TIMBER, CARVING, IRON-WORK, AND MAKING OF CARRIAGES,
WITHOUT BLOCKS, BOOTS, COACH-BOXES, OR WHEELS.

	Coach.			Chariot or Post-Chaife.			PHAETONS.									Curricle.			Gig.			Whiskey.		
							Large.			Middle.			Small.											
	£.	s.	d.	£.	s.	d.	£.	s.	d.	£.	s.	d.	£.	s.	d.	£.	s.	d.	£.	s.	d.	£.	s.	d.
Perch *carriages*, including the timber, &c. as above	24	15	0	22	5	0	20	0	0	18	0	0	16	4	0									
EXTRAS TO DITTO.																								
The fide of the perch plated with iron	3	3	0	2	15	0	2	10	0	2	2	0	1	16	0									
The perch made of a bent or compaffed form	1	1	0	1	1	0	0	18	0	0	18	0	0	16	0									
A whole-wheel front	2	10	0	2	5	0	2	0	0	1	15	0	1	10	0									
A half-wheel front	1	5	0	1	3	0	1	0	0	0	18	0	0	15	0									
Crane-neck *carriages*	41	0	0	36	18	0	33	10	0	29	18	0	26	18	0									
EXTRAS TO DITTO.																								
The cranes having double bows	3	3	0	2	15	0	2	10	0	2	2	0	1	16	0									
Two-wheeled *carriages*																15	0	0	11	11	0	9	0	0
The curricle, with fhafts for a temporary ufe																18	10	0						
The gig-made curricle, for frequent alternate ufe																16	0	0						
Whiſkey-made curricle																			13	0	0			

By this ftatement, the value of every kind of *carriage* is to be obtained, any way completed, by adding thereto whatever conveniencies or ornaments may be thought neceffary, and which are afterwards diftinctly treated of.

CARVING.

CARVING.

THIS art contributes more effectually than any other part of the work to the beauty and elegance of a town or state carriage. In common carriages, all that is meant by carving, and which scarcely deserves the name, is the finishing the ends of the timbers with scrolls, and the edges with mouldings. If any carving is bestowed on those plain carriages, it is on the blocks or raisers, whose front views are more conspicuous than any other timbers, and requires some degree of fancy to reduce their bulk to any agreeable appearance.

The only persons at variance with this art are the coachmen, who, from the greater difficulty of cleaning after use, resent the extra trouble they are put to, and with the mop and brush endeavour to destroy those ornaments with which the carriage is beautified.

On carriages for common use, the more simple and plain the ornaments are the better, so as a good design is but preserved, leaving the painter's pencil to effect what is omitted in the carving, which is a tolerable substitute in a common, but a very poor one in a superior, carriage. The carving being a necessary ornament to the timber-work, its value is always included, and proportioned to the quantity contained, and the excellence of its execution, and which muſt depend on the ſufficiency of the artiſt. The different repreſentations of blocks in Plate 12 will tend to give ſome information of the price of carving, as the timber-work is the ſame in expence for carved as for plain blocks: the increaſed amount on blocks is the conſequence of the ſuperior ornaments, which may be increaſed to any value.

CHAP. V.

IRON-WORK.

THE articles of this fort are excessively numerous, and are manufactured by a variety of different mechanics, such as spring, axletree, step, and tyre smiths, &c. which will all here be considered under one head, and the most essential articles treated of separately, without enumerating every trifling article that is occasionally used, and which would be almost impossible to select.

This, next to the timbers, is what ought to be particularly attended to, for the advantage of good materials and workmanship, which, together, greatly add to the preservation of the *carriage*. The whole of the iron-work requires to be made of particularly tough iron, and fitted with great exactness; taking care that each gives its proper support without straining or twisting, and that its substance be adequate to the weight it is meant to carry. All the external parts should be well filed, and formed in whatever shapes they may be required.

The iron-work forms, and is, the principal part of the *carriage*, both for value and ufe. Its properties cannot be too well attended to. For the purpofe, therefore, of giving every information on that material article, it is here feparately reprefented, although included in the former value and reprefentations where its connections with the timber are defcribed; but as many articles in iron-work would be found wanting to fome future alterations, the feparate value of the moft material or likely will be given apart from the timbers.

SECT. 1.

SPRINGS.

SPRINGS, by which only riding is made comfortable, require the greateft attention to their properties, otherwife their effect is materially injured. They fhould be all manufactured of a well-prepared fteel, properly tempered. The greater the number of pieces or plates there are, confined within the fize of the hoop, the better; and the longer the fpring is, the more eafy and elaftic its motion will prove. Thofe that are the leaft erect, and of courfe that incline most to the weight they carry, and that are also the longest from the bearing or stays, have a superior advantage.

Their forms are various, according to the purposes for which they are designed; and they are named according to their shape—such as the S, the C, the French horn, the scroll, the worm, the single and double elbow, or grafshopper spring, which are all shaped according to the situation in which they are to be placed.

The springs all support the weight at their extremities, by means of loops or shackles; and their elasticity is only from the hoops, at which part the plates are all made thickest, gradually tapering thinner to their extremities, and shortening about four inches in each plate from the hoop, where the bearing for the spring is fixed. Those that are placed in an erect form, are obliged to be supported with iron stays, which clip the spring at the hoop; those that are placed horizontally are supported from the middle, and play their whole length; those that are made of a circular form have frequently no stays, but are well secured at the bearings. Short, light springs, which contain but few plates, have frequently no hoops; but the plates are confined with a small rivet, and the bolts with which the spring is confined to its bearing.

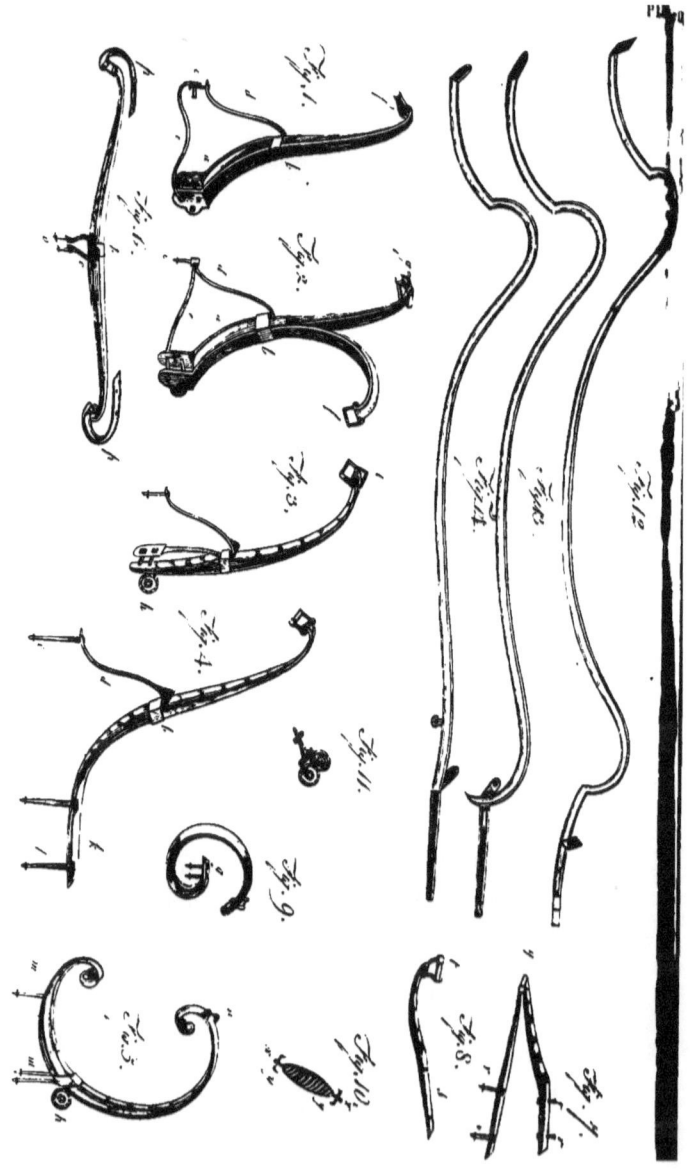

SPRINGS.

The variety of fprings in ufe could not all be reprefented, nor the different values of them afcertained with accuracy. What is reprefented in the plate will convey fufficient information of thofe generally now in ufe.

COACH AND CHARIOT SPRINGS.

Fig. 1. The ufual form of fprings ufed to carry the body of a coach or chariot. This is called an S fpring: it is made with a ftay *a*, which is rivetted within the hoop *b*, and clips at bottom the fore or hind tranfom, and is there fixed by this bolt *c*. and is fupported at the hoop by a ftay *d*, which refts on the hind axletree bed, or budget-bar; a ftay *e* alfo clips or bolts through the fpring at bottom, and clips or unites in a cup with the other; to oppofe the preffure, it has a fhackle *f* bolted loofely on the top, for the weight to hang by.

The difference in expence of thofe fprings betwixt coach and chariot, is on account of their different fizes; the coach has one or two plates more than the chariot, and is made fomewhat wider acrofs the back.

DOUBLE

DOUBLE SPRINGS.

Fig. 2. The form alſo of a ſpring for a coach or chariot: it has united to it at the back plate an additional ſpring, which turns the reverſe way, to carry ſeparate things with the body, ſuch as the budget before, or platform behind; having a double ſhackle at *g*, the one to carry the body, and the other the boot or platform, the reverſe ſpring has only to carry the hind part of the ſame boot or platform. The ſtays and loops, marked *a, b, c, d, e, f,* are for the ſame purpoſe as the former, the bottom ſtay being only differently formed; the former clips, and this cups on the bed or bar.

GIG SPRING.

Fig. 3. This ſpring carries the weight, and is fixed in the ſame manner as the others: the form is frequently uſed for either of the above purpoſes, but is here repreſented only as a gig or curricle hind ſpring, having a jack at the bottom *h*, and a double-loop ſhackle at the top *i* for the brace, which is fixed in it, and extends to the body-loop, from which it returns through the upper loop, and down the back of the ſpring, and is ſecured

secured in the jack at the bottom; this requires no stay at the bottom part, it being fixed on the bar near the shaft, which answers the same purpose.

LONG-TAIL PHAETON SPRING.

Fig. 4. This spring has a long flap *k*, and is supported on carved blocks, to raise and ornament them, on which blocks they are fixed by bolts, which pass through them and the cross-framed timbers. Those springs are obliged to be stayed on the inside, at the middle, and top, to prevent twisting sideways; they are supported at the hoop in the same manner as the rest, by a stay, which takes its bearings on the block.

SCROLL SPRING.

Fig. 5. This is a peculiarly formed spring for ease, and is used to various kinds of carriages. It rests, and is fixed on a long block for phaetons, or on the two bars only for coaches, &c. at the bearings *m m*; the bottom is sometimes turned up in a scroll form, for ornament only, in imitation of the upper part; the brace is hung by a shackle,

shackle, or placed round the spring, and, passing through a loop *n*, is fixed in a jack at the bottom.

GRASSHOPPER, or DOUBLE ELBOW SPRING.

Fig. 6. This is a spring used to light whiskies or chairs. It is fixed on the axletree by a Jew's-harp staple *o*, which staple is united with the spring-hoop, and bolts through the axletree; it supports the weight at each end by one or two loops *p p*, which are fixed at the bottom of the shafts; it is mostly fixed at the one end, but has room to play at the other. Those springs most generally have only one loop at the hind end, in which it is fixed, and the other end bears on a thin plate fixed to the bottom of the shafts.

SINGLE ELBOW SPRING.

Fig. 7. A pair of single elbow springs uniting together at the extremities by looping one on the other, and are there confined by a small round bolt: they sometimes have no hoops, but the plates are confined by a small rivet, and the two bolts *r r*, which fix them to their bearing places;

those

thofe are moftly defigned for phaeton or gig fore ends; frequently one of them only is ufed, having a loop in place of a double fpring.

LOOP SPRING.

Fig. 8. This is fometimes fixed on the end of the bottom fide, to carry the body, inftead of a folid iron body-loop; to give additional cafe to the rider: it is bolted on at the bearing *s*, and receives the braces at the fhackle *t*.

FRENCH-HORN SPRING.

Fig. 9. This is a circular fpring ufed to the fore part of a curricle or gig. Sometimes the brace fixes to a fhackle, but generally is placed round the back through the loop *u*, and is confined by the bolt *u*, which fixes the fpring to the fore bar.

WORM,

WORM, OR SPIRAL SPRING.

Fig. 10. This is a light, fquare piece of fteel, turned in the fhape of a barrel, which is placed between the double of the main brace, to give eafe to the paffenger in riding; it is fecured within the brace by two fcrews *x x*, having two plates *y y* placed between the fcrew and the brace.

SPRING JACK.

Fig. 11. This is a fmall engine fixed to the bottom of the fpring. Its ufe is to receive a brace when placed round the fpring, which brace is fixed to a fpindle that is turned with a wrench upon the outfide, and is there confined by a fmall ratchet-wheel and ketch. Its ufe is to heighten or lower the body.

PRICE

PRICE OF SPRINGS.

THE value of fprings is in proportion to their fizes. The fhackles, the bolts, the loops, and ftays, are reprefented with the fprings: and being of neceffity ufed with them, are included in the following ftatements: The jacks, though reprefented, being a matter depending on choice, are feparately valued. The general height or length of fprings is about three feet; and they are made light or ftrong, as may be found neceffary to fupport the weight of the body; and as the fame form of a fpring may be ufed to different *carriages*, ftating the value of two or three different fizes of each form that is ufed, will make the information fufficient for general ufe.

COACH OR CHARIOT SPRINGS.

Fig.		Coach. £. s. d.	Chariot. £. s. d.
1.	A pair of S-formed fprings, with fhackles, ftays, and bolts, complete	3 18 0	3 6 0
2.	A pair of double-returned fprings, to carry body and boot, fhackles, ftays, &c. complete	6 10 0	5 10 0
5.	A pair of large fcroll fprings, for a travelling carriage, with clips and fhackles complete	6 6 0	4 18 0
8.	A pair of fpring body-loops	1 15 0	1 10 0

PHAETON,

PHAETON, GIG, OR CURRICLE SPRINGS.

Fig.		Large. £. s. d.	Middle. £. s. d.	Small. £. s. d.
3.	A pair of whip springs for a curricle or gig —	3 10 0	3 3 0	2 15 0
4.	A pair of long-tailed high phaeton springs, with the front stay, shackles, and bolts — —	4 4 0	3 10 0	3 0 0
5.	A pair of scroll springs for phaetons — —	4 10 0	3 15 0	3 3 0
6.	A pair of grafshopper whiskey springs, with loops and shackles complete —	3 0 0	3 0 0	2 10 0
7.	A double pair of elbow phaeton fore springs —	1 15 0	1 10 0	1 5 0
7.	A single pair of ditto for loops — —	1 5 0	1 1 0	0 18 0
9.	A pair of French-horn springs, for a curricle or gig — —	1 15 0	1 10 0	1 5 0
10.	A pair of worm springs, screws and plates complete	1 10 0	1 5 0	1 4 0
11.	A pair of spring jacks —	1 0 0	0 18 0	0 15 0

In this statement, the value of almost every kind of spring, generally used, is ascertained. Their value is regulated by their length, to which also the plates are proportioned in number or thickness: upon an average, they may be computed at 1s. 6d. the inch for the small, 1s. 9d. for the middle, and 2s. for the large-sized springs; the measure to be taken from the bolt at the bearings to the centre of the top eye.

SECT. 2.

AXLETREES.

THE axletree of a carriage is made in one entire piece, and is fixed quite acrofs the carriage; that part between the wheels is called the bed, and that which goes through the wheels, the arms, which fhould be made perfectly round, and fomewhat ftronger at the fhoulder than at the end, which is moftly fcrewed to receive a nut, through which and the axletree the lince-pin paffes, to keep all tight. The nuts are made with a collar at the face, and a temporary collar or wafher is driven on to the back of the arms, which forms two fhoulders for the wheel to wear againft, and helps to preferve the greafe from running out, and to prevent dirt from getting in.

The axletrees are the principal or only fupport of the carriage, on which every attention and care fhould be paid to the felection of good iron, and to fee that they be well wrought, and of fufficient ftrength, rather going to the extreme than to rifk the life of the paffenger by the overfetting of the *carriage*, which moftly happens when an axletree breaks. By the axletrees alfo the wheels are regulated to any width at bottom, to fuit the track of the roads in which they are to run, and are confined to the *carriage* by means of clips, hoops, and bolts, which are all described in plate xi.

The shape of the axletree between the shoulders varies according to the situation they are placed in, or the form of the timber with which they are united; those are the most firm that are flat-bedded in the timber.

THE AXLETREE BOXES.

THOSE are frequently called long-pipe or wheel-boxes; they are long casings fitted close to the arms of the axletrees, and securely fixed in the wheel-stocks, or naves; they are usually made of wrought sheet iron, of a substance proportioned to the weight of the carriage: their use is to contain a supply of grease, to prevent the effects of friction, and assist the wheels in their motion. These succeeded the short cast-iron boxes, which, to *carriages* of this sort, are totally out of use, they being injurious to the axletrees by cutting them at those parts they wear against, so as to occasion a frequent lining of the arms, now never necessary on that account.

There

AXLETREES.

There are many forts of axletrees and boxes invented various ways, for the following purpofes: viz. for containing a longer fupply of greafe or oil, to be more durable, to fecure the wheels, and to leffen the draught.

Some of thofe inventors even pretend, that all thefe advantages are combined in one axletree; but the generality of thefe inventions extend to the advantage only of retaining a fupply of oil, and wearing a greater length of time than the others; but as it would not be juft to give any partial decifion on the merits of either, to the prejudice of the owners, by attending to the following obfervations on each, affifted by the reprefentation in plate x, the reader will be enabled to judge for himfelf.

In order to render the information complete, concerning each figure of the different axletrees in the plate, they are reprefented with each end or arm in different views: the one end fhews the axletree and the box whole, and feparate from each other; the other reprefents the axletree, with its box, nuts, and caps united, horizontally cut through the middle, for the purpofe of fhewing the infides thereof.

THE COMMON AXLETREE AND BOX.

Fig. 1. The common fort of axletree and box is moſt generally uſed, being ſimple and cheap, in compariſon with the others; the box is what only wears, and is frequently obliged to be refitted to the arms, otherwiſe they give to the wheel, while in uſe, an unſteady motion, and ſoon exhauſt their ſupply of greaſe. Thoſe, if well fitted, will contain their ſupply for about one week's regular uſe, or a journey of one hundred miles. They wear at the rate of one ſet of boxes to every two ſets of wheels; and require, in that time, to be twice or thrice taken out of the wheels, and refitted to the axletree arms.

A. The arms of the axletree, which are made round, but rather of a conical form; ſtrongeſt at the back or ſhoulders *a*; tapering to the lince end *b*, which is ſcrewed for a nut, and alſo has a ſmall hole for a lince-pin *c*, which prevents the nut from coming off: at the body end is a collar or waſher *d*, for the back of the wheel-ſtock to wear againſt.

B. The box whole and half ſhewn. This box is made of ſheet iron, proportioned in ſubſtance to the weight or ſize of the axletree, having the

ſhutting

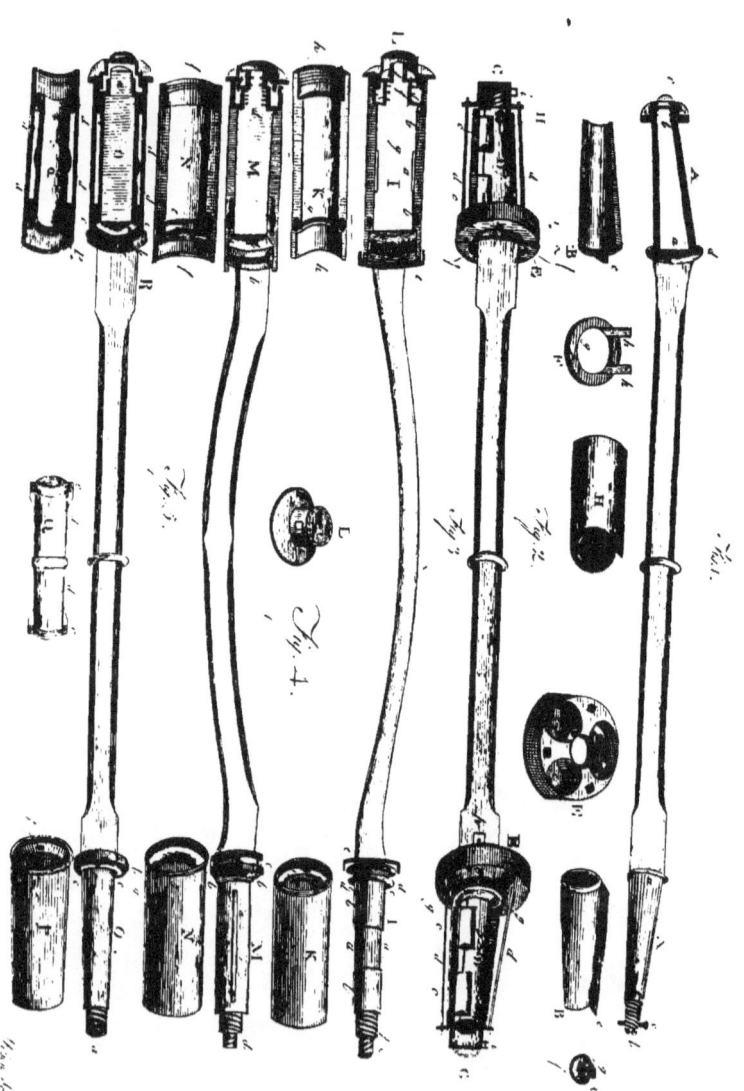

Plate X

shutting edges *e* welded in a ridge, which secures the box in the wheel.

C. The nut, which has a broad face *f*, to lie flat against the wheel, and is tapped or screwed to receive the screw end of the axletree; each of those nuts turn on the screw the same way the wheel goes, and have a notch *g* for the lince-pin to pass through, for the purpose of securing the nut from turning off.

THE PATENT ANTI-ATTRITION AXLETREE AND BOX.

THE advantages which this axletree and box are pretended to possess over the common sort, are very great, principally lying in the great relief given to the draught, the retention of oil, the ease with which it is replenished, the great security for holding on the wheels, and their durability. Those axletrees, if made with the security for the wheels, need no nut or lince-pin, as in those on the common principle.

D. The arm of the anti-attrition axletree represented whole at both ends, to give the different views of the reservoir, the strap washer, and rollers, with the box on each arm, as horizontally cut through the middle. Those axletrees at bottom are reduced from a perfect round, and grooved to receive two rollers *c c*, on which the weight of the carriage is borne, in order to facilitate the motion. These rollers form the circumference of the bottom of the axletree, which is reduced to make the weight rest only on them.

E. The reservoir, or concealment for the oil, being closely fitted and fixed by three bolts *d d d*, on the back of the wheel-stock; containing the oil within three recesses *e e e*, which oozes through small channels on to the arm of the axletree, which it supplies for a considerable time: it is made of cast metal, and has a cap *f* projecting behind, which prevents the dirt from getting in.

F. The wheel-security, or strap-washer; this has a collar *g*, which is placed within the wheel, between the reservoir and stock, and has, fixed to the collar, lugs or straps *h h*, which extend backwards some distance on the bedded part of the axletree, where it is fixed by a nut-screw: by means of this strap-washer, the wheel is secured to the bedded part of the axletree.

G. The cap, which is also fixed on the front part of the wheel-stocks by three bolts *d*; and by means of a screw-plug *i*, the axletree and reservoir is replenished with oil.

H. The box, which is of the same form as the common box, only made of a very hard metal, of a thickness proportioned to the weight of the carriage;

carriage; this also shews how the axletree is supported on the rollers, and prevented from bearing on the arms.

THE PATENT CYLINDER AXLETREE AND BOX.

Fig. 3. The advantages of this axletree and box over the common sort, are principally in the length of time they wear; the silent and steady motion they preserve to the wheels; the advantage of retaining the oil to prosecute a journey of two thousand miles, without being once replenished.

Those axletrees and boxes have gone through some considerable improvements since their origin, and have met with such encouragement, that it has induced other persons to copy them so nigh as scarcely to admit a decision in favour of either, except that experience has proved in the one what can only be suggested in the other; but, from every circumstance. they appear to possess the same advantages.

I. The axletree arm, made as perfectly cylindrical as possible, and of a peculiar hard surface; the middle *a* reduced, to contain the oil necessary to feed the axletree at the two bearings *b b*, having a shoulder *c*, against which the wheel-box takes its bearings; the adjoining collar *d* is grooved for a washer, to preserve the oil, and prevent noise in its use, with a rim *e* on the collar of the axletree, to answer the use of a cuttoo. The end *f* is double screwed, to receive two nuts for securing the wheel; the one screw turns the way of the wheel, the other the reserve, and is meant as an additional security to prevent the wheel coming of.

K. The box shewn whole, and horizontally cut through the middle, which is made of a very hard metal, nicely polished, and fitted to the arms; having a recess *g* at the back part, for containing there a supply of oil; having back and fore end projections *b b*; the back one fits close to the rim of the collar, which it covers; the fore one projects without the surface of the wheel-stock, and is screwed on the inside, to receive the screw of the cap.

L. The cap, which covers the nut, and receives the waste of oil, is mostly made of brass, and screwed on, or in the box, and against the front of the wheel-stock. This form of cap is used to all but the common axletree.

THE NEW PATTERN CYLINDER AXLETREE AND BOX.

Fig. 4. This new invention has some ingenious evasions of the patent, but encroaches so much upon its principle as to make it unnecessary to bestow further observation on them; but where they are different, a sufficient description is given in the plate; and its references will convey as much information as is consistent with impartiality.

M. The arms, made as perfectly cylindrical as possible, of a hard surface, having a shallow flute or groove at *a* on the top, for the oil to be conveyed to the extremity of the axletree, which it continually supplies.

The collar or shoulder *b* is made conical for the wheel box to wear against, having a small groove also at *c*, for receiving a leather to prevent noise in use; a leather washer is also applied between the box and shoulder; it has also a double-screwed end *d*, to receive the nuts, which are also screwed on reverse to each other: in the form of this screw there is also a little difference made, only as a deviation from the copy.

N. The box shewn as whole and horizontally cut through the middle. This box is also made of a very hard cast metal, nicely fitted and polished within. The recefs for the oil at *e* is the fame with the laft, as alfo are its projections *f* for the fame purpofe exactly, except the back fhoulder, which is bevelled to fit the conical collar.

THE NEW PATTERN AXLETREE, WITH DOUBLE CASE BOX.

Fig. 5. This new invention, the novelty of which lies in the box, is for the fame purpofes as the two laft, to contain a fupply of oil, and wear perfect for a greater length of time, than the common axletree and box. This, in the conftruction, differs much from the reft, but the want of time to prove its fufficiency prevents any certain recommendation.

O. The arms of this axletree are made in the fame manner as the common fort, but cafe hardened, with a fingle fcrewed end *a*, having a brafs collar *b*, with a deep groove *c*, to receive the projecting end of the outward cafe box which runs therein, and prevents dirt getting between the axletree and box.

P. The outer box or cafe, with the wearing box within, reprefented whole, and horizontally cut to fhew the principle of it.

Q. The

AXLETREES.

Q. The inner or wearing box shewn apart, previous to fixing it in its case. This box is made case hardened on the inside, and fits closely to the axletree arms; they are made shorter than the case or outer box, to admit the projection *b b* at each end for the same purposes as the last, having two collars or bearings *c c*, which fit close to the inner surface of the outer box, between which two bearings and boxes at *d d* the oil is contained, which oozes through two small holes *e*, at the back end of the box, on to the axletree arms.

These two boxes, after being made separate, are welded or brazed to each other; the oil is supplied at the back through a small hole *f*, which is plugged with a cork or screw.

R. The collar, made of brass, is fixed on the back part of the axletree arms, having a groove *g*, in which the back projection of the outer box is to run, for the purpose of preventing dirt from getting in.

Each of those three last axletrees have peculiar wrenches to take off the nuts and caps with, and which are always included in the price with them.

PRICE

PRICE OF AXLETREES.

THE value of common axletrees and boxes is neceffary to be known apart from the carriage, that any alteration for thofe of the patent fort may fhew the exact difference of expence, whereby the preference may be judged of with more certainty. The common axletrees are valued by their weight, which, from each fize to the other, leffen about one-tenth—from the large coach to the fmall phaeton, in proportion to the former ftatements of carriages. The other forts of axletrees are not fo regularly reduced in the prices, but are ftated according to the fancy of the proprietor. The value of the boxes are included with thofe axletrees, but not with the common fort; when new boxes become neceffary, the prices of them, and putting in the wheels, are ftated feparately.

PRICE OF AXLETREES.

FOR A FOUR-WHEELED CARRIAGE.

	Coach.	Chariot.	PHAETONS.		
			Large.	Middle.	Small.
	£ s. d.	£ s. d.	£ s. d.	£ s. d.	£ s. d.
Axletrees, per pair	3 10 0	0 3 3 0	0 2 17 0	0 2 12 6	0 2 7 0
Boxes, per set	1 16 0	0 1 12 0	0 1 10 0	0 1 8 0	0 1 6 0

FOR A TWO-WHEELED CARRIAGE.

	Curricle.	Gig.	Whiskey.
	£ s. d.	£ s. d.	£ s. d.
Axletrees, each	1 15 0	1 11 6	1 8 0
Boxes, per pair	0 15 0	0 14 0	0 13 0

The patent and new-pattern axletrees and boxes are reduced in their expence to three sizes only—the coach, chariot, and phaeton; but in this the proprietors are not all regular in the allowance, some charging the same price for the axletrees and boxes of a phaeton as others do for those of a chariot: they however all allow the single axletree, for curricle, gig, or whiskey, to be regularly half the price of the cheapest pair. The statement is nearly as follows:

	Coach.	Chariot.	Phaeton.	Single for Gig
	£ s. d.	£ s. d.	£ s. d.	£ s. d.
Patent anti-attrition axletree, per pair	21 0 0	0 20 0 0	0 19 0 0	0 9 10 0
Patent cylinder, ditto	27 16 0	0 26 5 0	0 26 5 0	0 13 2 0
New pattern, ditto	23 0 0	0 22 10 0	0 22 10 0	0 11 0 0
New pattern, with double box, ditto	26 10 0	0 26 10 0	0 24 10 0	0 12 4 0

By this statement, the value of any change of axletrees to a new carriage is known. The alterations to old carriages for any pattern, must have the expence of taking out and putting in added.

SECT. 3.

CRANES.

CRANES are the ſtrong iron bars to which the hind and fore part of a carriage on each ſide are united. They are made of a crooked form, reſembling, at the fore part, that of a crane's neck, for the purpoſe of admitting the fore wheels to paſs under unobſtructed, whereby ground is ſaved in turning, which gives to carriages made with them a great advantage, as they can be uſed with more freedom in narrow, confined places, and have alſo a great ſuperiority in the appearance, in any handſome carriage. They require to be manufactured of the beſt materials and workmanſhip, as they ſupport, like the perch, all the weight of the body: they are different in their forms, which makes alſo a difference in their price, and which has before been ſtated under the head of Crane-neck Carriages in page 67, which makes it quite unneceſſary to give any further account of them than what is repreſented in Plate IX. Fig. 12, 13, and 14.

Fig. 12. The double-bowed crane, having the hind part ſhaped in imitation of the fore part, which fills up the vacant ſpace behind, and forms a more agreeable line to the ſhape of the body.

Fig.

Fig. 13. The half-bowed crane, bent on the hind part to imitate the double bow, which bend extends to a bearing on the axletree-bed.

Fig. 14. The common crane, having only the neceffary bend for the wheel to lock under, from which bend it continues almoft ftraight to the hind end.

SECT. 4.

STAYS.

STAYS are iron bars, varioufly formed, and of different defcriptions, taking their name from the effential part which they are meant to fupport: fome of their bearings are by collars, and then are called collar-ftays, alfo when a collar is wrought in the middle of a bar for ornament. Their ufe is very great, to confine or fupport any two feparate parts of the carriage, which is done by being wrought with collars, fhoulders, clips, or fpurs, and are confined by bolts to their fituations: there are many of thefe ftays which are called irons, which are lefs neceffary to fupport, and take their name from the parts to which they are applied; of which fome are lightly fixed, and others are only frames for leather coverings, &c.

Thofe

Thofe being articles of iron-work which form a part of the carriage, are included in their value; all that is neceffary, is to reprefent them in the plate, and explain their ufe. When any of them require to be repaired, or replaced through failure, the prices will be found under the general article of Repairs.

The fpring ftays are all reprefented in plate x. with the fprings, fhewing how they are fupported at the hoop, and likewife the manner of fixing the ftays to the oppofite refting-bar, with clips, flaps, or cups.

PLATE X.

A. The bottom or main ftay of a curricle or one-horfe chaife; it fupports the fhafts from the axletree, to which it is alfo confined, is fixed on the bottom of the fhafts, and unites the bars by means of lugs or clips croffing the joint.

B. The horn-bar ftay, which, bolted at the middle, on the bottom of the perch, is carried up to the end, and fixes to the horn-bar, which it ftrengthens, to fupport the preffure of the fpring ftays.

C. The coach-box ftays: the ftraight one is the back or ftandard ftay; the crooked one, the

compafs

compafs or foot-board ftay, which fupports the foot-board: the other prevents the coach-box from coming forward, by being bolted to the horn or budget bar.

D. The hind ftandard ftays, are the ornamental guard-irons fixed on the hind part of the carriage; the back and front ones are fometimes both of one fhape; their ufe is to fupport the upright ftandards, to form a part of the ornament, and prevent other carriages coming too clofe behind.

E. The feat-irons, by which the coachman's feat is fupported and fixed by means of a cradle, which ties or buckles on to the loops at the ends; they are fixed in the ftandard at the top, and are hooped and bolted thereto.

F. A luggage-iron, or budget-frame; this frame, after being bolted on to the bottom of a platform, is covered all over with leather, and forms the fide of the boot.

G. The dafhing-iron; a frame for a gig or curricle, which is covered with leather for the purpofe of avoiding fplafhing in travelling; it is bolted through the fore bar, and is generally fupported from the back by two ftays, having loops at the ends for affiftance to mount by.

H. The wheel-irons, of different fhapes, the ftraight and compaffed. The compafs wheel-irons are for the purpofe of forming a ftep or tread

Vol. I.   H

tread for the coachman to mount on; the straight ones are used to post-chaises; their use is to stay the splinter-bar where the draught is taken from, and to which it hooks on at the socket eye, and fixes on to the axletree end against the wheel, where it is secured by the axletree-nut.

I. The wing iron, or frame for the wings of a chaise, which is covered with leather, and fixes on the elbow-rails.

K. A head frame, to which the head of a chaise is fixed, when intended to be taken off occasionally.

SECT. 5.

PLATES.

PLATES are material articles of the iron-work, as they add to the strength and preservation of the timbers; in particular where they are curved, or where any two parts wear against each other.

L. The perch side-plate, of which there are two to a perch, are fixed on to the sides of the timber, to which they are secured by rivets: they admit the timber to be reduced, which gives a much lighter appearance to the carriage, and prevents

vents it from fettling by the weight of the body, as the other perches will do.

M. A bottom-plate, which is bolted flatways to the bottom of the perch, to affift the timber in its ftrength; thofe are not ufed with fide-plates, but a fhort piece, called a wearing-plate, is fixed on the bottom of every perch for the fway-bar to wear upon.

N. The tranfom-plates, of which there are two, are made flufh to the top of the fore axle-tree-bed, and to the bottom of the fore tranfom, to ftrengthen and preferve the timbers from wearing by the friction they are neceffarily fubjected to in turning of the fore carriage.

O. The half-wheel plate; a flat, femicircular plate, horizontally placed, and united with the fore tranfom-plate, and is cafed on the top of the circular part with a wood moulding; its ufe is to maintain a fteady bearing to the locking of the fore carriage.

P. A whole-wheel plate; a circular plate, horizontally placed between the fore bed and tranfom; it is fufficient in its bearings without a top tranfom-plate, as it preferves an equal bearing on any lock of the fore carriage; a fmall wearing-plate is neceffary on the centre of each bed. Thofe wheel-plates are always ufed to crane-necks, and frequently to the better fort of perch carriages; they are cafed on the top like the half-wheel plates, with a wood moulding.

Q. The fway-bar plate; fometimes ufed to ftrengthen the fway-bar, and preferve it from wearing by its friction againſt the wearing-plate of the perch, but is fometimes wholly omitted, or has leather fubſtituted in its place.

R. The nofe-plate, which is a ſhort plate bolted and clipped acrofs the bottom of the futchels, to keep them ſtiff for the pole, which refts alfo on it.

S. The ſtandard-plates, are plates bolted on the back and front of the coach-box ſtandards at the bottom; they clip, and are fixed to, the tranfom: by means of thefe plates the coach-box is fixed: the plates fometimes extend up to the bottom of the ſtays, to ſtrengthen them.

T. The crofs-key plate, is bolted acrofs the top of the futchels, and preferves their ſtrength againſt the ſtrefs of the pole, which it fupports at the back end, in a contrary direction to the nofe-plate at the fore end.

U. The boot door-plate, a broad, thin plate, which is fcrewed over the ſhutting edges of the door, as a rabbit to ſhut againſt.

V. The futchel-plate, a thin, fquare plate funk in a level with the chap of the futchel, to preferve the hole from wearing by the pole-pin.

W. The

W. The pump, or guard-handle plate, is a plate screwed on the bottom of the timber to strengthen it.

X. The short-block plate, is a plate for the same purpose as above.

Y. A corner-plate, a bent iron used to strengthen the joints of any framing.

SECT. 6.

SOCKETS OR CAPS,

ARE iron ferrules, fixed on the ends of the timbers, either for strength, or for instruments to draw by.

Z. The shaft-sockets; are sockets wrought in the bottom plate of the curricle-gig for the shafts, which are occasionally used for one horse; they are placed in those sockets, and confined by a screw.

a. A splinter-bar socket, mostly made with an eye, wrought from the solid, in which the wheel-iron is hooked.

b. The small splinter-sockets, shewing the hook, the eye, and dragon's-tongue, which are for one and the same use, that is, to fix the traces to, for the purpose of drawing by.

c. The pole-cap or ring, is a ring-focket fixed to the extreme end of the pole, with loops for the pole-pieces, which are placed therein.

SECT. 7.

HOOPS AND CLIPS,

THOSE are ufed for uniting two feparate things together, in order to ftrengthen each other; the hoops confine them by being forcibly driven on, and the clips by being fixed with bolts; they are made of tough, thin iron, and formed to the fhape of what they are defigned to unite.

d. A perch hoop, which unites the wings to the perch, by being tightly drove over them.

e. An axletree-hoop, which is forcibly drove on the axletree and bed, to confine them together at the fhoulders.

f. A clip which is placed over the axletree, and fecures it in the bed to which it is bolted, and is alfo ufed for other purpofes.

g. A clip, which fecures the fhafts of a one-horfe chaife to the fore-bar, through which it is bolted.

SECT. 8.

BOLTS, NUTS, AND SCREWS.

THOSE are the principal inftruments by which the timbers and iron-work are confined to each other: they are made of various lengths and fizes, but moftly of half an inch diameter, and of differently-formed heads, faftened by a fcrew or nut at the bottom; which nuts are proportioned to the fize of the bolts, and are of a fquare form, in general, to be fcrewed on by a wrench; fome are made for temporary purpofes, to be fcrewed on with the finger and thumb, and are called thumb-nuts; fometimes a fcrew with a ftrong thread, and a head made like a nut, fupplies the place of a bolt, and is called a nut-headed fcrew.

h. A perch-bolt; a ftrong, iron pin which goes through the centre of the fore axletree-bed and fore tranfom, and is what the fore or under carriage is fecured by to the upper one, and by which bolt the carriage turns and is drawn; a fmall key or pin goes through the bottom, or it is otherwife fecured by a fcrewed nut.

i. The common bolt, which receives a fcrewed nut at the bottom, and is ufed to fix moft of the work together.

BOLTS, NUTS, AND SCREWS.

j The common nut, which screws on to the bolt, and what it is fastened by.

k. A collar-bolt; a bolt with a shoulder or collar in the middle and double-screwed ends, which serves to fix one thing upon another, that either may be separately taken away without displacing the other.

l. A strap-bolt, with a thumb-nut, having a flat part with holes, by which the bolt is fixed to the side or top surface of any timber, and is mostly used to secure the door or lid of boots.

m. A pole-pin; a round, iron pin with a flat head, by which the pole is kept in its place.

n. A splinter-bar roll, or roller-bolt, a long bolt with a large, round, flattish head; the upper part is fixed through a roll of three inches deep, and two diameter, leaving the bolt of such a length as to fix through the splinter-bar and futchel, or splinter-bar end only; its use is to receive the traces by which the carriage is drawn.

o. A tee-headed bolt, with a thumb-nut, is a bolt with a head made in the form of a T, to fasten the ends of a short brace between two separate things, which is done by contracting the brace in the middle; mostly used to the bar of a curricle or chaise; to hang the splinter by.

p. The bolt hook and eye, are two bolts having projections from their shoulders, one of which is wrought in a hook, the other in an eye, to receive

ceive it: they are used to separate things which occasionally hang together; mostly used to the shafts of a one-horse light phaeton.

q. A nut-headed screw; a large, thick screw, with a strong thread, to hold well in the timber, and a thick, square head, in the form of a nut, to be screwed on with a wrench: they are of various lengths and sizes, and their use is to fix any two strong parts together.

r. A trunk-fastener, is a strong screw, with a collar and square head, used for the purpose of keeping a trunk steady on the platform.

SECT. 9.

RINGS, STAPLES, LOOPS, AND SHACKLES.

THESE are instruments by which other things hang or are confined: their form and substance vary very much from each other, according to the separate purposes for which they are intended.

s s s. The body-loops, made to various patterns, to fix at the bottom corners of the body, by which it hangs to the spring: they are made of a strong substance, and are wrought with a square loop to receive the main brace.

t. A body-loop for a gig, which hangs from the pillar, through which it is bolted, having a spur or stay without, and a strong stay within, to preserve the pillar.

u. A shackle, which bolts on to the top of the springs, to which it hangs, and receives the brace from the body-loop.

v. The body-loop, with stay and spring, united: mostly used to a step-piece body.

w. A double and single collar-brace ring; the double ring is made with a square loop at each end to receive the collar-brace, and is fixed on the top of the perch; the single ring is made with one loop, and fixes to the bottom of the body.

x. A check-brace ring; a ring made with a strong screw, to fix in the middle of the corner pillar for the check-braces to loop through.

y. A pole-staple; a large, iron staple drove into the top of the pole at the back part, and which receives the gib to keep the pole tight.

z. A breeching-staple; a staple which screws in the shaft: it use is to receive a breeching-strap of a one-horse harness, to which it is buckled.

1. A shaft-hook and a shaft-tug, two things which are meant for the same purpose; that is, to receive the bearing-tugs of a one-horse harness.

2. A pole-hook, a strong, long hook, fixed on the end of a pole, by means of two bolts in a plate: its use is to hang the middle splinter-bar to, when four horses are used.

3. A Jug-

3. A lug-hook, which is a plate turned at the top, having holes on the fides to fcrew it to the fide or end of a trunk, by which it hangs.

SECT. 10.

JOINTS AND PROPS.

BY joints is to be underftood the iron-work by which the heads of chaifes, landaus, phaetons, &c. are fixed up or let down; and the props are what the ends of thofe joints are fixed upon and fupported by.

4. A joint for a landau head, which is fixed on two props only.

5. The joint for a chaife or phaeton head, which is obliged to be double, and fixed on three props.

6. The bottom, top, and middle props, for the joints to be placed on, and which are fecured by a nut: the bottom prop fuftains the main purchafe, and is the ftrongeft.

7. The neck-plates, which are feparate, thin plates, made to fcrew on each of the flats; they are all placed on each fide a bolt, on which the head is made to act.

SECT.

SECT. 11.

STEPS.

THE steps in this representation are only those of necessity, and which are included in the value of the carriage already mentioned. The double and treble steps, requiring more than the iron-work to make them complete, are hereafter treated on, and their separate value affixed.

8. A footman's step; this step is fixed to the hind part of a carriage, having a back stay thereto, to strengthen it.

9. Single steps to a one-horse chaise carriage, &c. having also the stays, shewing the two principal forms they are made in.

MANY of those articles of iron-work are unconnected with the bodies and carriages already stated; but they compose a part of the additional and following requisites, in which their value is also included; such as the boots, coach-boxes, &c.; but they are here represented, to make the knowledge of them more complete.

CHAP.

CHAP. VI.

WHEELS.

UPON the superior advantage given to the motion by the different heights of the wheels, opinions are frequently divided; some maintaining the large, others the smaller wheel. On smooth ground the smaller wheel moves quicker than the large; but on a rough or uneven surface, the large wheel has the preference, as it will easily overcome the resistance which obstructs the small one.

Wheels should be made, to four-wheeled carriages, as near of a height as the construction and appearance will admit; and if not required for heavy work, the lighter they are made the better. The fixtures, from whence the draught is taken, should be placed rather above the centre of the largest wheel, for advantage of draught.

The members of a wheel are of three descriptions, viz. the nave, the spokes, and the fellies. The nave is the stock, made of elm, in which all the spokes are fixed, and in which the axletree or wheel-box is confined, to receive the axle-arm.

arm. The spokes are straight timbers, made of oak, firmly tenoned in the nave, and are the support of the fellies or wheel-rim. The fellies, made of ash or beech, are the rim of the wheel, which is divided into short lengths, in the proportion of one to every two spokes: those are fixed on the spokes; and, on them, the iron or strakes, which maintains the wear, are nailed.

The height of the wheels regulates the number of spokes and fellies that they are to contain; as the larger the circumference of the wheel is, the number of spokes required is greater in proportion; they should not be, to any wheel, more than fifteen inches apart on the fellies between the spokes.

The usual height of wheels extends to five feet six inches, and are divided in four proportions, to contain from eight to fourteen spokes, and only half that number of fellies; and are reckoned eights, tens, twelves, or fourteens, which are the number of spokes in a wheel, or fellies in a pair. The height, which regulates the number, is, for an eight-spoked wheel, not to exceed three feet two inches; for a ten, four feet six inches; for a twelve, five feet four inches; for a fourteen, five feet six or eight inches. These are the extreme heights for the different number of spokes to each wheel, which should be rather more than less, in particular to the fore wheel of a four-wheeled carriage, which

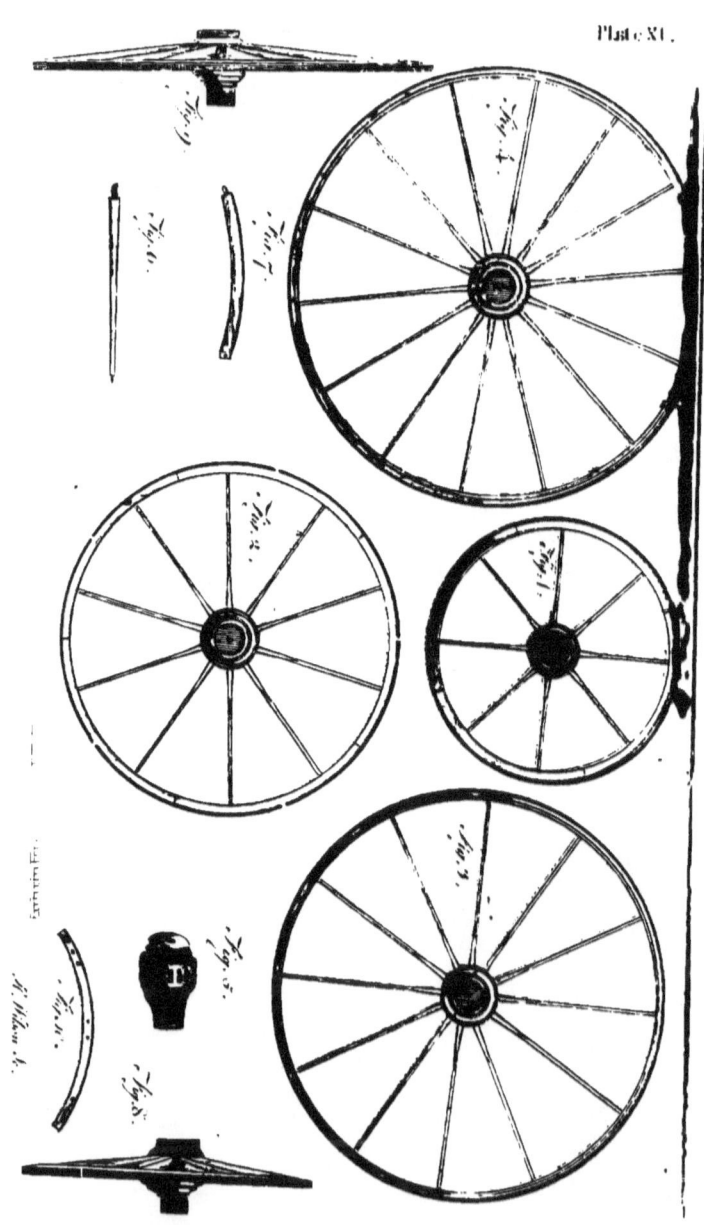

Plate XI.

which receives more ſtreſs than the hind one; and the rule is, when the hind wheels are of that height to require fourteen ſpokes, the fore one, if under the neceſſary height before ſtated, ſhould have twelve; never allowing the fore wheels to have but two ſpokes leſs than what is needful for the hind ones.

There are three deſcriptions of wheels, viz. the ſtraked, the hooped, and the patent rim: the difference of either is only in the rim; ſo that in wheels there are four heights, and three ſorts, which make twelve different prices in the whole, ſuppoſing them all of one ſize; but as they are made lighter for phaetons and chaiſes than for coaches and chariots, the prices vary accordingly.

PLATE XI.

Fig. 1, 2, 3, and 4, are wheels of four different heights, ſhewing the number of ſpokes each wheel ought to contain, and the difference of the three ſorts now generally uſed, the hoop, the ſtrake, and patent rim.

Fig. 1. A hooped wheel, called an eight, made with fellies, and hooped on the rim with an entire piece of iron.

Fig.

Fig. 2. A ſtraked wheel, called a ten, made on the common principle, with fellies, and the iron rim made in ſhort lengths, called ſtrakes.

Fig. 3. A hooped wheel, called a twelve, with fellies, and a hooped rim of one entire piece.

Fig. 4. A patent wheel, called a fourteen; this is the patent rim, made of one piece of timber, ſhewing the nuts and bolts with which the rim is faſtened.

Fig. 5. The nave, or ſtock, which is the centre of the wheel, in which the ſpokes are fixed.

Fig. 6. The ſpoke, which fixes in the ſtock, and ſupports the rim.

Fig. 7. The felly, ſhewing the pins or dowels on the end, by which it is kept ſecure at the joints.

Fig. 8. The ſide view of a ſtraked wheel.

Fig. 9. The ſide view of a rimmed hoop wheel.

Fig. 10. The ſtrake, which is the ſhort iron with which the common wheel is rung.

THE

THE PATENT OR BENT-TIMBER WHEEL,

HAS the rim of one entire piece, bent to the circle, inſtead of ſhort lengths, or fellies, which are hewn to the ſhape; the ſtrength of the bent timber is preſerved while the other is deſtroyed; beſides, it is hooped with iron, inſtead of being ſhod with ſtrakes, and will often laſt twice the time longer in wear than the others will do, has a much lighter and neater appearance, and on that account is often preferred.

The mock patent, or hooped wheel, comes very near the others in appearance and uſe, particularly if made with aſh fellies; as the preſervation of both lies in the hoops that the wheels are rimmed with. It is compoſed of part patent and part common, having the timber the ſame as the ſtrake, and the iron as the patent wheel.

The common ſort of wheels are preferred by many of account of their being more eaſily repaired than the hooped or patent wheel, which is certainly right; but, though the repairing of them is more difficult, yet they are much leſs ſubject to need it.

PRICE OF WHEELS, PER PAIR, OR SET.

Number of Spokes to each Wheel, or Fellies in the Pair.			Straked.	Hooped.	Patent.
Fore Wheels.	Hind Wheels.		£. s. d.	£. s. d.	£. s. d.
	Twelves and Fourteens	COACH	7 10 0	8 10 0	11 11 0
Setts. {	Twelves and Fourteens	CHARIOT	6 16 0	7 17 0	10 17 0
	Tens and Twelves	LARGE PHAETON	6 12 0	7 12 0	10 12 0
	Eights and Tens	MIDDLE-SIZED DITTO	5 11 0	6 6 0	7 7 0
		SMALL DITTO	4 10 0	5 5 0	7 0 0
Pairs. {	Fourteens	CURRICLE	3 10 0	4 4 0	5 15 0
	Twelves	GIG	3 2 0	3 14 0	4 14 0
	Tens	WHISKEY	2 11 0	3 3 0	4 0 0

When the fellies, or rims of wheels, are moulded, which they sometimes are, an additional charge must be made. In general, the various heights of wheels regulate the extra charge; but, when required to be made much heavier for a coach or chariot, a proportionate addition in the price must be made of 18s. in the set.

	Coach, Chariot, or Large Phaeton.	Middle or small-sized Phaeton.	Curricle, Gig, or Whiskey.
	£. s. d.	£. s. d.	£. s. d.
For moulding the fellies	0 19 0	0 17 0	0 10 0
Heavy wheels for a travelling carriage	0 18 0	—	—

Those prices do not include the painting, for the difference of which see *Supplement*, page 49.

BOOTS OR BUDGETS.

SECT. 1.

BOOTS OR BUDGETS.

BOOTS and budgets are moftly underftood as one article, though fo differently called : they are all intended for one purpofe, which is that of carrying luggage, and are moftly fixed on the fore part of the *carriage*, between the fprings: that wherein the principal difference lies, is made with a loofe cover, and is properly the budget, being made convenient for trunks; thofe budgets, for travelling carriages, or common poft-chaifes, are, by far, the moft ufeful ; the others are boots, of a trunk form, made more fquare, and are moftly ufed for town carriages, but can be of no other advantage than that of carrying loofe hay, horfe-cloths, &c. From one or other of thefe boots, conveniencies are fometimes made for the fubftitute of a coach-box, to fave labour to the horfe when the carriage is ufed for poft-work, or to preferve the view from within uninterrupted by a coach-box and hammercloth.

Boots are frequently ufed at the fore end of phaetons, and then moftly have the fore fprings fixed thereto by means of carved blocks, which are bolted to their fides, and ufually have the ftep for the entrance to the body fixed or hung thereon. Boots and budgets are fometimes ufed to the hind part of travelling carriages, but more frequently ufed to the hind parts of phaetons, gigs, or curricles, and are of two fizes lefs than what are ufed to coaches or chariots; they are all fo near in form as to make the defcription given in the plate fufficient for the general purpofe of information.

PLATE XIII.

Fig. 1 and 4. Are the common, fquare, japanned boots, moftly made of thick elm, and covered with ftrong ruffet leather, welted round the fides, opens in the front with a door, which has an iron plate fcrewed round the edges for it to fhut againft, and is faftened by means of a bolt and thumb-nut, or private lock.

Fig. 2. A platform, or luggage boot, made as the fkeleton is reprefented in Plate VII, with iron-framed fides, which are here, in Plate XIII. reprefented covered with a ftout black-dreffed leather, over which the cafe or cover, made of the fame, is placed, and buckles to the fides, back, and front; the borders of which fhould be welted to the top-piece, as they fit much better than when made of one piece of leather, as they ſometimes are. Within thoſe budgets are ſtraps fixed to the bottom, to confine whatever is placed in them, which otherwiſe would be injured by the motion of the *carriage*.

Fig. 3. A boot made with a convenience for the coachman to ſit on to drive; this boot requires to be made much ſtronger than the others, owing to the weight of the man, and, to make it eaſy to him, may be hung upon ſprings, as repreſented; which ſprings alſo carry the body. This boot ſhould be framed of ſtrong aſh, and boarded for the leather, with half the top to throw up to a perpendicular poſition by means of two irons of a ſemicircular figure, which run in a groove or ſtaple fixed in the framing, and are confined, when up, by a thumb-ſcrew on each ſide; on the inſide of the top is made the ſeat, which takes up but little room in the boot when down; the front lets quite down, but is ſtayed, to anſwer the uſe of a footboard, by means of two hinged, flat ſtays fixed by the ſame ſcrews as the irons are; it is faſtened, when down, by the bolt on the front paſſing through a plate on the top, and ſecured by a thumb-nut; thoſe are readily placed, and ſhould have a door to open behind, if the ſeat is to be made fixed.

Fig. 4. A phaeton boot; this boot is made ſimilar to Fig. 1, but not of ſo ſquare a form, but is obliged to be made rather ſtronger, on account of receiving the weight of the fore part of the body, which is fixed to the springs that are bolted on blocks to the sides; this has always a step on the sides, from which, sometimes, other steps are to hang; they sometimes open at the top, and sometimes at the back or fore ends.— For *the Salisbury Boot, see Coach-boxes.*

Coach, chariot, and large phaeton boots or budgets, vary so little in their size as to make the difference in value not worth notice: the sizes beneath those are two, and are used to gigs, curricles, middle and small-sized phaetons; so that, on the whole, they may be considered as of three proportions, which usually are as follow:

	Long.	Wide.	High.
Large size,	3 ft. 0 in.	2 ft. 3 in.	1 ft. 6 in.
Middle size,	2 ft. 3 in.	1 ft. 8 in.	1 ft. 3 in.
Small size,	1 ft. 6 in.	1 ft. 2 in.	1 ft. 0 in.

PRICE OF BOOTS AND BUDGETS.

	Large.			Middle.			Small.		
	£.	s.	d.	£.	s.	d.	£.	s.	d.
A platform or luggage budget, as Fig. 2. — —	8	0	0	6	0	0	4	0	0
A trunk-boot, as Fig. 1 and 4	5	0	0	3	10	0	2	10	0
A framed trunk-boot, to open with a feat for the coachman, as Fig. 3 — —	10	0	0	9	0	0	8	0	0
A ditto framed, for a coach-box to be placed on, as in Plate XIV. Fig. 3. — —	6	0	0	4	6	0	3	3	0

Those are supposed to be all made on one and the same principle, only reduced in their sizes, and the statement will answer to every kind of carriage; and any that come within or between those sizes may easily be ascertained hereby: but if any of the platform-budgets are made with wood sides, instead of iron frames covered with leather, as the small boots frequently are, then one-fourth may be deducted from their value.

CHAP. VII.

PLATFORMS, or RAISED HIND and FORE ENDS, and BLOCKS.

THOSE platforms, raifers, or blocks, are added to a *carriage*, either as matter of neceffity or appearance, but moftly for appearance, being generally ornamented with carving in different degrees; their ufe is to elevate and fupport the budget, boot, hind foot-board, and fprings; they are generally placed on the fide of the carriage, and relieve the infide framings from being obfcured by the platforms, as they are lightened and moulded, and give to the carriage a more airy appearance: being of various defigns, they are all omitted from the former charge of the naked carriages as ftated, fo that any defcription may be added according to fancy.

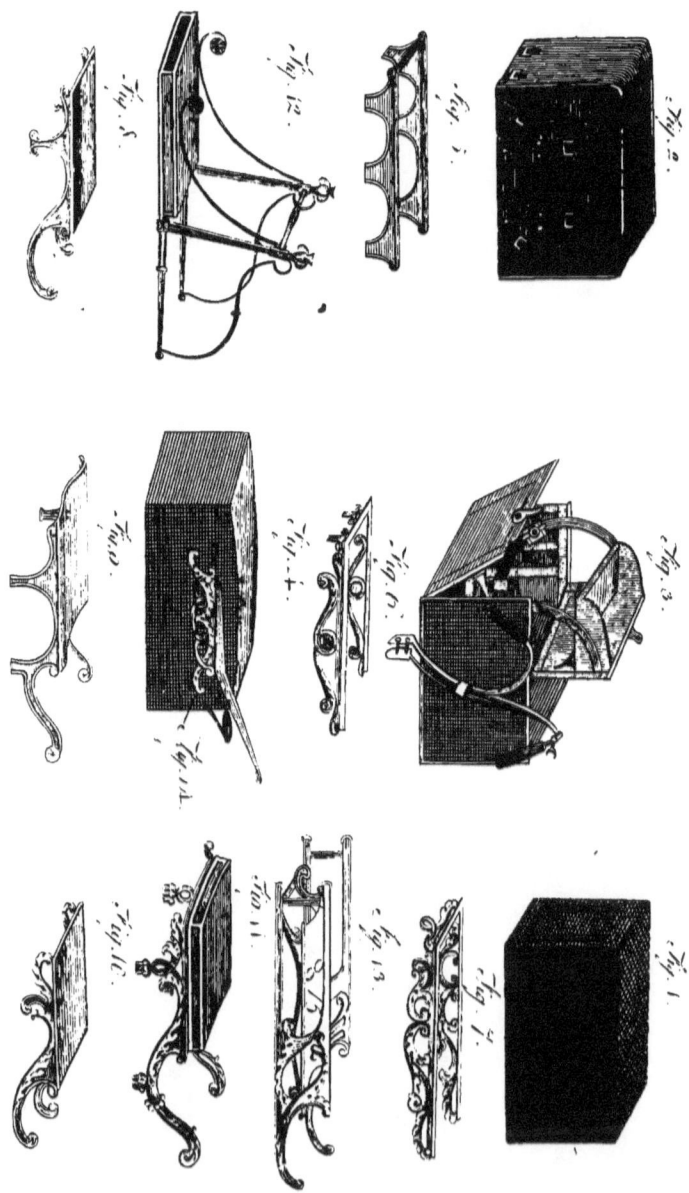

SECT. 1.

RAISED HIND ENDS, PUMP HANDLES, AND SHORT BLOCKS.

Fig. 8, 9, 10, 11, 12, 13, 15. Thofe different forts of hind ends are for one and the fame ufe, viz. for relieving the platform or footboard from the hind framings to whatever height is neceffary: the difference is, that the pump, plow, or guard handle, (Fig. 9, 11, and 12) are made to extend in the form of one of thofe handles mentioned, and are ftrengthened by iron plates; thefe ferve for the fervant to help himfelf up by, and to keep the horfes of other carriages from coming too near to do injury to the pannels. The fhort blocks (Fig. 8 and 10) are what are ufed to poft-chaife *carriages*, or to fupport a platform for ftandards; they do not extend further from the hind fpring-bed than what ferves to ornament them.—The phaeton and chaife blocks (Fig. 15) are of various forms. If the hind end is narrow, with two bars only, they are made like the fhort blocks; but, if wide, for long fpring blocks, they extend to the furtheft bar to fill up the great fpace, and form a large platform for a trunk, &c. to be placed on occafionally.

SECT.

SECT. 2.

RAISED FORE ENDS, OR FORE BLOCKS.

Fig 5, 6, and 7. Those fore blocks are the same to the fore ends, as the others are to the hind ends, to raise the budget or boot, and relieve the framings, in order to assist the appearance of the fore part of the carriage: those mostly have their bearings across the framings between the springs; there is also a fore bar, on which one of the bearings rests, that is frequently called a block, but can only be considered a block when ornamented to answer the sides; it bears a proportion in value of about one-fourth of the other two; so that, when omitted, it may be deducted from the amount given, which includes it.

SECT. 3.

SPRING BLOCKS.

Fig. 13 and 14. Spring blocks are of two sorts, which materially differ from each other; the one is to raise the hind springs, the other the fore ones; and, like the others, are more or less ornamented; but those represented are of the largest

largeſt and ſuperior kind, from which they may be reduced to any pattern. Long blocks or platforms are frequently fixed between them when a hind budget is not uſed, for the purpoſe of filling up a large vacancy acroſs the bars.

SECT. 4.

CUSHIONS AND STANDARDS.

Fig. 11 and 12. Footman cuſhions were intended to make the ſituation of the ſervant more comfortable, but are now ſeldom made otherwiſe than in the form of a cuſhion, with boards only, covered with leather, without any ſort of ſtuffing, to make them more eaſy than a common footboard: their chief uſe is to raiſe the footman, and to ornament the *carriage*, particularly when ſtandards and wings are added to them, which are alſo aſſiſted in their ornament and ſtrength with the irons that ſupport them. The carving introduced in thoſe ſtandards is alſo a great addition to their appearance; and they are at preſent the principal ornaments to the hind part of a *carriage*. Their advantage, beſides ornament, is to prevent other carriages coming ſo cloſe behind as to injure the ſervant or pannels.

PRICE

PRICE OF RAISED HIND AND FORE ENDS, BLOCKS, STANDARDS, AND CUSHIONS.

THOSE articles are the same in value whether to a coach or chariot *carriage*, for which they are principally used. The difference in their price arises from the manner in which they are ornamented; and to state them finished in the three different ways, as are represented in the plate, will furnish sufficient information of the general variety now in use.

	Plain Moulds.			A little ornamented.			Much ornamented.		
	£.	s.	d.	£.	s.	d.	£.	s.	d.
Fig. 9 and 11. A pair of pump, plough, or guard-handle blocks and footboard	2	0	0	3	0	0	4	0	0
Fig. 8 and 10. A pair of short blocks and footboard	1	10	0	2	5	0	3	0	0
Fig. 5, 6, and 7. A pair of raised fore end or budget blocks	1	10	0	2	10	0	3	10	0

	Plain.			Plated round the top.			Plated top, bottom, and corners.		
Fig. 11. A footman-cushion only	2	2	0	2	18	0	3	16	0
Fig. 12. A footman-cushion with hind standard	6	0	0	6	18	0	7	18	0

	Large.			Middle.			Small.		
Fig. 13. A pair of hind spring-blocks for a phaeton	4	4	0	3	3	0	2	2	0
Fig. 15. A platform for ditto raised with blocks	1	10	0	1	5	0	1	0	0
Fig. 14. A pair of fore spring-blocks only	1	0	0	0	15	0	0	10	0

With those articles, the expence of putting them on, and the materials used, are included in the above statements.

CHAP.

CHAP. VIII.

COACH-BOXES.

A HANDSOME coach-box is a great ornament to a carriage. Of thefe there are various forts now introduced, inftead of riding poft, to fave unneceffary burden to the horfe, and fatigue to the driver, which are two very material objects. The objection by many perfons to a coach-box, is the obftruction it gives to view; but they may be fo adapted as not materially to affect the fight from the front windows; and any convenience, however fimple, is by far better than fatiguing both man and horfe; but, to carriages ufed in town, a fubftantial coach-box is indifpenfably neceffary, as it affords fo material an advantage to the driver; nor is the view from the front fo great a matter of concern as if intended for country ufe.

SECT. 1.

STANDARD COACH-BOX.

Fig. 1. This coach-box is the moſt general and ſimple in uſe, as it is light, and convenient to remove on any occaſion; it is moſtly preferred for thoſe carriages that are alternately uſed for town and country: they are ſimply fixed by means of plates, which clip the tranſom, and are ſtayed on the hind or boot bar, and fixed with collar-bolts.

SECT. 2.

THE SALISBURY COACH-BOX.

Fig. 2. The Saliſbury boot, though of a bulky and heavy appearance, is by far the moſt convenient and faſhionable coach-box in uſe: it is boot and coach-box together; and although it be apparently heavy, it is not more ſo than the common coach-box and boot, together, as the inſide is all a cavity, which is peculiarly convenient to carry parcels in, or to contain the coachman's requiſites, having a large, flat bottom,

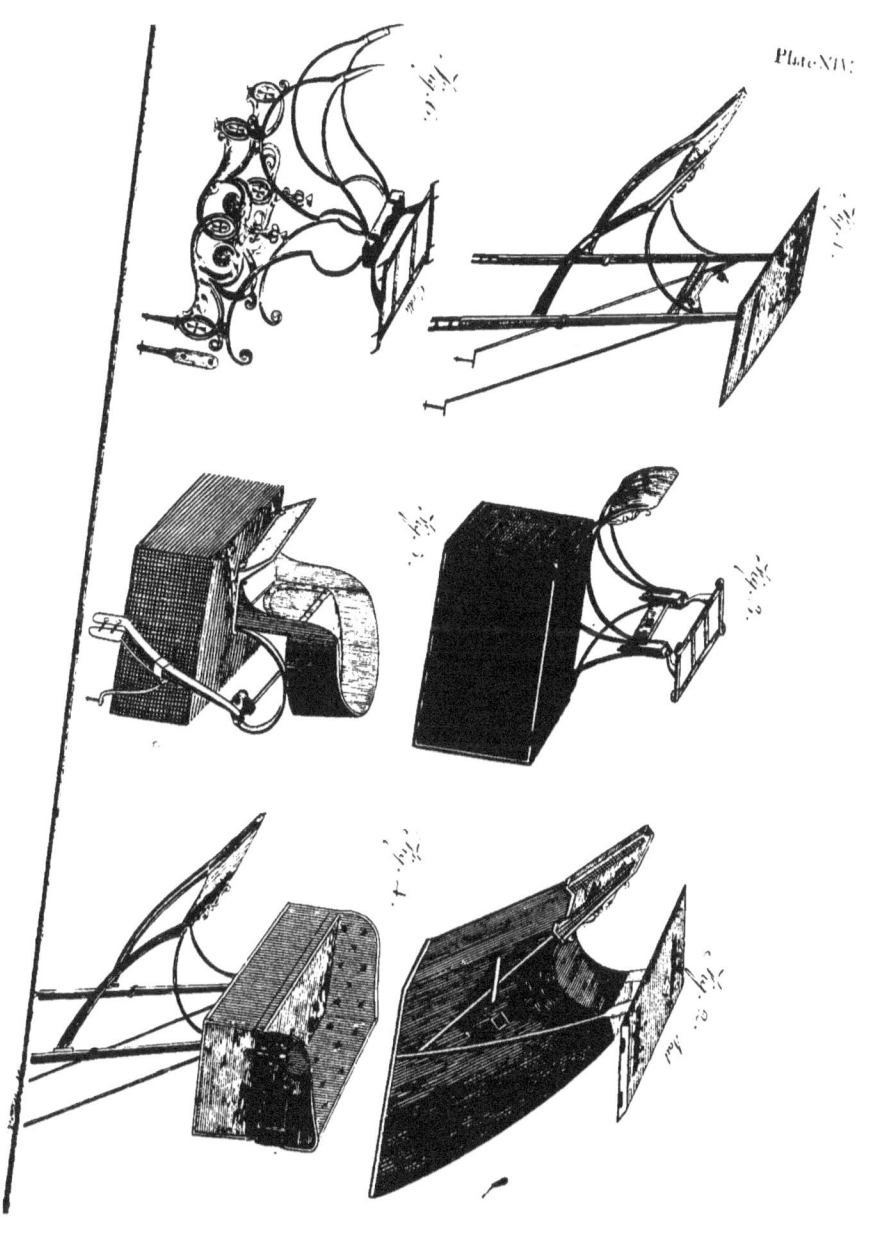

tom, which, resting on the framings or blocks, makes it more steady than other coach-boxes on the common principle. This sort, however, is not so convenient to remove, and requires, when taken off, to have the vacant space filled by another kind of budget, such as is usually put on to post-chaises.

SECT. 3.

IRON COACH-BOXES.

Fig. 3 and 6. The iron coach-boxes are of the most agreeable design, of a very light appearance, but are more heavy than the others. They are made to fix on the top sides of a boot, or are supported on rich ornamented blocks: they can easily be taken off from the boot; but from the blocks it is never necessary, being only used to handsome town carriages. Their form differs agreeable to the fancy of the builder; but are mostly of either of those designs that are represented; the one shewing the footboard, and brackets or ledges on, and the other without them.

SECT. 4.

TRAVELLING COACH-BOXES.

Fig. 4. The difference of this coach-box lies in the feat only, is principally used for travelling carriages, but which may be made to any of the three laſt-deſcribed coach-boxes, though moſtly uſed to the one repreſented: it is made with iron frames at the ends, covered and lined with leather all round, with a cuſhion of the ſame, and has leather falls, which anſwer the purpoſe of a hammercloth: it is fixed on to the top iron-work with bolts, having a cradle, the ſame as the others, for the ſeat; they ſometimes hang upon ſprings, and are made with a head and knee-flap the ſame as to a one-horſe chaiſe; their uſe is to make the ſituation of the ſervant more comfortable, and more ſecure from danger, when travelling on bad roads: they can be made ſo as to take off occaſionally, and have the uſual ſeat and hammercloth put on.

SECT. 5.

THE CHAISE COACH-BOX.

Fig. 5. This is made in imitation of a chaife body, and occafionally placed on the boot; is of a fize for one or two perfons to fit in, frequently intended for the proprietor's own pleafure to drive, or to give more freedom to view from the front windows. They fhould always be lined with leather, and hung fo as to be eafy to ride in; a pair of fprings fhould be fixed to the front part, and hung or fixed to the boot; the hind parts fhould be fupported from thofe fprings which carry the body, by means of a bar which croffes them, having the loop of the coach-box made to encircle this bar, and to hang thereon with a fhort brace. This kind of a coach-box may be made to fix on a one-horfe chaife carriage, and ferve both purpofes; but if for this purpofe only, it is ufually made much more fimple than the one defcribed.

sect. 6.

THE COACH-BOX SEAT AND CRADLE.

COACH-BOXES are not complete without cradles and seats; but as, on some occasions, they may be separately wanted, the separate statements will therefore be necessary, and their value may be added to the coach-box.

A cradle is a leather platform, made to receive the seat: it is fastened to the loops on the seat irons, and is either buckled or tied thereon, so as to let loose or tighten at pleasure. By those cradles the seating for the coachman is made comfortable, and is generally adapted to their several conceits.

The seat is a long-formed cushion made of various sizes, but mostly two feet three or four inches, by three feet ten inches, or four feet long, made of strong canvass and leather, stuffed with straw, and covered over with cloth or baize, lined at the bottom ends with strong pieces of leather, called galling-leathers, which rest on the seat-iron, and preserve it from wear by rubbing thereon. It is fixed on the cradles by straps which pass through it towards the ends, which straps are fastened to the fore standards. Sometimes those seats are fastened to the seat-irons

irons with ftraps and buckles; the feat-irons then extend to the width of the feat, which has two fquare holes in each end for the ftraps to go through: this method gives more length to the cradle, and makes the feat fink in the middle by the coachman's weight, whereby it is more eafy to ride on.

PRICE OF COACH-BOXES.

	£.	s.	d.
A common coach-box, as Fig. 1.	3	15	0
A Salifbury ditto, as Fig. 2.	8	15	0
An iron ditto, as Fig. 3. and 6.	8	10	0
A framed boot for ditto,	5	5	0
Carved blocks for ditto, as Fig. 6.	8	8	0
A chaife-box without the boot, Fig. 5.	10	0	0
A coach-box budget, as Plate xii. Fig. 3, the fprings excepted	10	0	0

SEATS AND CRADLES.

	£.	s.	d.
A common cuſhion feat	0	18	0
A cradle and ftraps for ditto	0	12	0
A travelling coach-box feat fixed on the feat-irons, as Fig. 4.	3	13	6
A ditto with fprings	7	7	0

SECT. 7.

TRIMMINGS.

THE trimmings about a carriage, with which the cloth is ornamented, have, within thefe few years, been much increafed, both in quality and quantity. Therefore, to afcertain the value of linings or hammercloths with any accuracy, it is neceffary to reprefent the various forts of trimmings in ufe. That which is moft generally ufed is made of worfted, with narrow filk ftripes or lays, and is two inches and a half in width; from that it extends to three, three and a half, or four inches; but, for extraordinary purpofes, fuch as hammercloths, it will run to eight or nine inches.

The quality and breadth make a difference in the price. It is frequently made of cotton mixed with worfted; and fometimes, for very fuperb carriages, it is made of filk only. There are other forts of very narrow laces made, fuch as are ufed to feam the cloth with, or to cover the nailings; the one is called feaming, the other a pafting lace; the colours of which are made to match thofe in the broader patterns, but cannot form much of the figure, on account of the width. The pattern or figure of lace makes no difference

of

of expence, when the arms or creſt are worked in them, and then of courſe are extra, on account of the difference in workmanſhip. Fringes have alſo been greatly improved upon, and, like the laces, are to be valued according to their width and quality; as alſo if ornamented with button-hangers, which are moſtly put on them with a very good effect. The common width of fringe, including the gimp head, is five inches and a half. To form any ſtatement of the different prices of hammercloths and linings, it will be firſt needful to ſtate the ſeparate prices of the different ſorts of lace and fringe, and then the value of any hammercloth or lining may be collected from the quantity uſed on either occaſion.

PRICE OF LACES.

Inches Wide.		Worsted. per y.rd. s. d.	Worsted & Cotton. per yard. s. d.	Silk only. per yard. s. d.
2	Figure	1 4 —	1 8 —	4 0
	Crest	2 0 —	2 4 —	4 8
	Arms	2 8 —	3 0 —	5 4
2½	Figure	2 0 —	2 4 —	6 0
	Crest	2 3 —	3 0 —	6 8
	Arms	3 4 —	3 8 —	7 4
3	Figure	2 8 —	3 0 —	8 0
	Crest	3 4 —	3 8 —	8 8
	Arms	4 0 —	4 4 —	9 4
3½	Figure	3 4 —	3 8 —	10 0
	Crest	4 0 —	4 4 —	10 8
	Arms	4 8 —	5 0 —	11 4
4	Figure	4 0 —	4 4 —	12 0
	Crest	4 8 —	5 8 —	12 8
	Arms	5 4 —	5 8 —	13 4

Besides those broad and binding laces, there are some very narrow, that are invariable in their size, called seaming and pasting-lace; and also small trimming, called roses and French strings. The seaming is what the cloth is seamed with; the pasting is what covers the nailings of the cloth; the roses are what go round the holes of the cloth where

FRINGES.   135

where the hand-holders are placed; and the French ſtrings are what the glaſs-ſtrings are held by.

	Worſted.		Cotton.		Silk.	
	s.	d.	s.	d.	s.	d.
Seaming lace, per yard	— 0	6	— 0	6¼	— 1	8
Paſting ditto, ditto	— 0	5½	— 0	6	— 1	6
Roſes, per doz.	— 3	6	— 4	0	—16	0
French ſtrings, per pair	— 2	0	— 2	6	— 6	0

If, on any occaſion, a ſmall quantity of broad lace is required of any particular pattern, and a loom is neceſſary to be ſet for it, an expence is incurred from 10s to 20s. according to the pattern or width, beſides the price of the lace. The leaſt quantity a loom can be ſet for, without a charge, is 20 or 24 yards of broad lace.

———

SECT. 8.

FRINGES.

SILK fringes are ſo ſeldom uſed, that any obſervation on them is unneceſſary. Thoſe of any ſignification are what are uſed to hammercloths, and are of two ſorts, the plain and ornamented, (ſee Plate xv. letter *b*) and are uſually of the

following

following width and prices. The value of the ornaments called button-hangers, which are afterwards put on the fringe, is proportioned by the number of buttons on each hanger, which is regulated by the depth of the fringe.

PRICE OF FRINGES.

	Plain Worsted Fringe. Per Yard.	Worsted and Cotton Fringe. Per Yard.	Number of buttons to each hanger.
	s. d.	s. d.	
5 inches deep	2 8	3 4	3
6 ditto	3 4	4 0	4
7 ditto	4 0	4 8	5
8 ditto	4 8	5 4	6
9 ditto	5 4	6 0	7

The ornaments or hangers, to either fringe, exactly double the price, allowing six hangers to a yard.

SECT. 9.

HOLDERS AND STRINGS.

BY holders and strings are meant the lace, which is made up with tassels, and lined with cloth or leather, for the purpose of holding by, or drawing

ing up the glasses with; they are usually made of a greater width than the other lace, with which the lining is trimmed.

In a complete trimming, there are three descriptions of holders or strings, viz. the hand-holders, the swing-holders, and the glass-holders, or glass-strings, (see Plate xv. letters *a*, *b*, *c*) each of which is the same in value; these are called inside holders. There are, besides, outside footman-holders, which buckle on the back part of the body for the servant to hold by, sometimes used in sets (or four) and sometimes in pairs only: These holders are not always made of lace, but frequently of a strong wove worsted, called a webbing, in which only the colours, and not the figure, can be worked; these are the cheapest and most durable, but the lace-holders accord best with the other trimmings.

To state the price of holders, a reference must be had to the value of the different sorts of lace, adding to the quantity of lace used for each holder the price of the trimmings used to complete them, such as the tassels, the plated buckles, and the leather billets, with which they are made, to hang on the staples behind.

Every inside-holder takes a yard of lace, and every footman-holder a yard and a half.

The expence of making up the holders, with lining, tassels and buckles, is equal to the price of

HOLDERS AND STRINGS.

of the plain lace; fo that doubling the value of the lace, gives the price of the holders: but where the creft or arms is worked in the lace, the value of the taffels, &c. is only to be added to the amount of the figured or plain pattern lace—for example, one yard and a half of lace for a footman-holder, two inches and a half wide, at 2s. per yard, is 3s. worth of lace; the taffel and the billet and buckle to complete it, is alfo 3s. which makes 6s. for a holder of this defcription. The fame breadth and quantity of lace, with the arms worked thereon, is worth 5s. and the trimmings, &c. only 3s. which makes for this pattern-holder 8s.; fo that a pair of worfted lace footman-holders, two inches and a half wide, common figure, is 12s.; if with arms worked in the lace, 16s.

PRICE OF HOLDERS.

Inches Wide.		Inside hand-holders, and glass-strings. s. d.	Footman holders. Of lace. s. d.	Of web. s. d.
2	Worsted	2 8	4 0	3 0
	Cotton	3 4	5 0	4 0
$2\frac{1}{2}$	Worsted	4 0	6 0	4 0
	Cotton	4 8	7 0	5 0
3	Worsted	5 4	8 0	5 0
	Cotton	6 0	9 0	6 0
$3\frac{1}{2}$	Worsted	6 8	10 0	6 0
	Cotton	7 4	11 0	7 0
4	Worsted	8 0	12 0	7 0
	Cotton	8 8	12 0	8 0

Web-holders are usually made with worsted only, because the cotton so soon foils.

From these statements of trimmings, the value of every description of hammercloths or linings is to be obtained by first knowing the quantity necessary to be used, which is hereafter mentioned.

CHAP.

CHAP. IX.

PLATE XV.

THE LININGS AND INSIDE FURNITURE OF BODIES.

THE lining the infide of a body requires fome attention to give it thofe advantages neceffary for a gentleman's carriage. A richnefs in its ornaments is the moft material thing; and the difference of expence, which is principally in the lace, is fo trifling when compared to its ornamental advantages, that it would never have been confidered an object, had it been fully known. The colours of the cloth make no difference in the value, except fcarlet or crimfon, which make an addition of exactly one-third in the price of the cloth.

Thofe generally ufed for clofe carriages are light-coloured cloths; thofe for open carriages are of dark, or mixtures. The cloths fhould always be of the very beft fecond, if not fuperfine; but fecond is what is moftly ufed. The quilting

Plate XV.
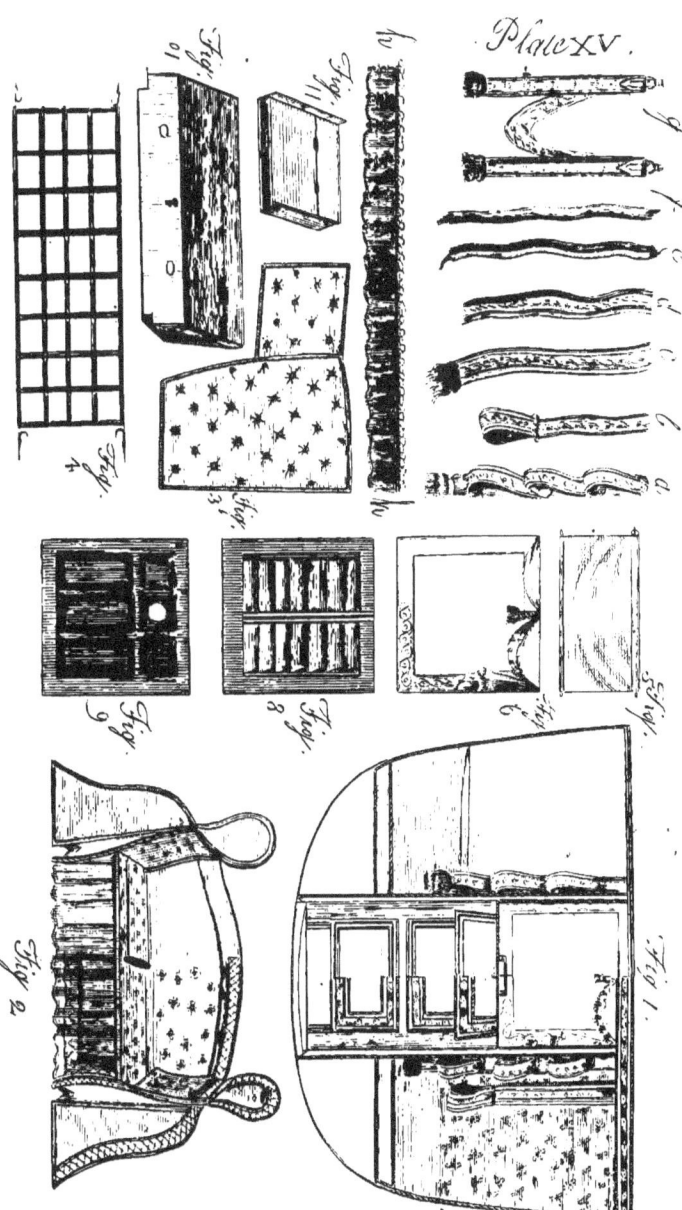

FURNITURE OF BODIES. 141

of the cloth with small ornaments, called tufts, also gives a richness to the lining; those should match the colours used in the trimmings; and the trimmings should be of such colours as are used in the liveries, but of any fancy pattern. The crest or arms lace has a noble appearance; but if the width of it exceed three inches and a half, it looks heavy. A fullness of cloth to the seat-falls should always be allowed, and a lace of two inches and a half breadth for the holders used on the plainest occasions; that for binding the falls, pockets, &c. two inches; but as the value of different trimmings can only be known by a separate description of the ornaments used, a reference to them will be found very necessary.

SECT. 1.

Letters *a, b, c, d, e, f, g, h,* (Plate xv.) represent the various trimmings with which the linings and hammercloths are ornamented, and, on account of the variety, are each described by small letters.

a. The hand-holders, are the loops for the hands to hold by, made of a yard and a quarter of lace, cut in short lengths, and nailed on the standing pillars, through part of the lining and
oval

LININGS AND INSIDE

oval trimmings, called rofes; a flat taffel ornaments the bottom piece.

b. The fwing-holder, a long loop for the arm to reft in, made of a yard and a half of lace, with an ornamented button to loop in different holes, ufed inftead of having elbows to project within the body.

c. The glafs ftring, or holder, is what the glafs is drawn up by, made of a yard of lace, ornamented with a flat taffel at the one end, and nailed on the glafs frame at the other; having button-holes worked, by which the glafs is hung to any agreeable height. All thofe holders are lined with a thin leather, or cloth, the fame as the lining; the glafs-holder has a narrow lace, called a French ftring, faftened to it, which, when the glafs is up, keeps it from the bottom.

d. The binding lace; the lace of different widths, with a tape edge, which the falls, the pockets, and the ftep linings are trimmed or bound on the edges with; the valent round the roof edge is made of this lace.

e. The pafting-lace, is a narrow lace of about an inch wide, with a taped edge. Its ufe is to nail the taped part over the other nailings of the cloth, and turning the lace fide over, which is palled down, covers all the nailings.

f. The feaming-lace, is a narrow lace of about half an inch broad, having a tape edge on each

each fide. This lace is fewed round a fmall cord, and then fewed in the corner feams of the cloth, and alfo nailed round the edges of the doors or windows.

g. The footman-holders; thofe are conveniencies for the fervants to hold by, which, if made of lace, are of two pieces, 3-4ths of a yard long, fewed together for ftrength; but if made of web, are double and left open, being ftronger: they are each ornamented with round or flat taffels, according to the width. The double holders are four in number, the fingle two; but the fingle pair has moftly a piece hanging acrofs between the two; they are made up with leather billets and buckles, and are buckled on to ftaples fixed on the back.

h. The fringes, which are feldom ufed but to hammercloths; one half is reprefented plain, and the other ornamented with button-hangers.

Fig. 1. The infide view of a coach body reprefented two ways trimmed; the one half fhews the plain method of trimming, the other the full ornamented.

The plain fide has the pockets, the falls, and valents, trimmed with a narrow two-inch lace, and the holders with a two and a half. There are many linings ufed plainer than this; but agreeable to the prefent fafhion, this is as plain as a
lining

lining ought to be, and fhould be an eſtabliſhed rule to go by.

The ornamented fide has the pockets, falls, and valents trimmed with a broad three inch lace, of the fame width with the holders, having alfo an extra fide or fwing-holder for the arm to reſt in. The fides are quilted with fmall ornaments, made either of cloth or worſted. It fhews a feſtoon curtain, and the glafs frame covered with lace inſtead of cloth.

Fig. 2. The infide view of a chaife lining, reprefented with red doors, to fhew the fides and back trimmings thereof. The plain fide of this body has the wings and falls bound only with a narrow inch and a half trimming; but there are many chaife linings that have no lace round thofe parts, further than that which the cloth is feamed with; but that is a very plain and ancient method of finifhing.

The cufhion to the plain trimming is reprefented only in one length, with a cufhion for the driver to fit on. The ornamented fide fhews the back wings and fides trimmed with a broad two inch and a half lace; the back and fides quilted the fame as the coach; the falls are bound with a narrow, and trimmed above with a broad lace, which is the method frequently ufed of trimming the falls of other linings.

The

FURNITURE OF BODIES.

The cushion for this is divided, the one half on the seat, the other is placed on a box for the driver to sit on; which cushion must also have a fall, trimmed the same as the other, to cover the box.

SECT. 2.

Fig. 3. A squab, or sleeping cushion; a thin cushion faced either with leather or silk, stuffed with soft wool, and quilted; they are occasionally added to the insides of close carriages, for the head or shoulders to incline against; they are sometimes made faced on both sides with leather and silk, to be used alternately. Those for the back part are generally made of a smaller size, extending only half the depth of the side one; they are usually bound with a narrow lace or silk ribbon, and fitted on with buttons or strings.

SECT. 3.

Fig. 4. A net; a convenience sometimes placed across the roof between the doors, for the purpose of containing light parcels free from injury.

They are made either with narrow thin lace, like a tape, or with worsted line; and may be fixed, or occasionally hung on hooks, as described.

SECT. 4.

Fig. 5. The spring curtain; a silk curtain fixed to a long barrel, containing a spring, which admits the curtain to be drawn down to an agreeable depth, and, by means of a trigger, is instantly drawn up to its place. A stick is sewed in the silk at the bottom, with loops at the ends, for the line to pass through; which line steadies the sudden motion of the curtain. These things are so convenient, that they are indispensably necessary to almost every kind of close carriage. The Venetian blinds are substitutes for them in a great measure, but that only when the glasses are not wanted to be put up.

SECT. 5.

Fig. 6. The festoon curtain; a silk curtain trimmed with silk fringe; mostly intended for ornament only, being found inconvenient for use; they are fixed over the lights or windows of the doors

doors as reprefented, and are fometimes made to hang in a drapery form on the fides, but moftly are ufed to the top only. They ornament very much the infide of a carriage, but are of no utility otherways.

SECT. 6.

Fig. 7. The glafs and glafs frame: the glafs frame is made of thin oak; the one fide is reprefented covered with lace, the other with cloth, in the ufual way. The glafs fhould always be of the beft plate; but a great difficulty lies in procuring them, particularly of Englifh manufacture: the French are the beft in ufe. The preferable glaffes are thofe which are free from bladders or veins; but, to clear them from thofe faults, they are frequently reduced to little more than the fubftance of crown or common window-glafs. It is almoft impoffible to feleɛt them free from bladders; but veins fhould never be admitted to pafs. Their value is only to be rated by their fize, excepting if diamond cut, or bevelled round the edges, which is now out of fafhion.

SECT. 7.

Fig. 8. The Venetian blind; a blind frequently ufed as a fubftitute for the common fhutter and fpring curtain, anfwering either purpofe, with the preferable advantage, in hot weather, of admitting the air and excluding the fun, and, when clofed, ferves the purpofe of the fhutter, to prevent duft from foiling the carriage while ftanding by. It acts by means of a fpring bolt, with which it is opened to any extent at pleafure. It is moftly painted a verdigrife green, but fometimes, to handfome carriages, is painted of variegated colours, and varnifhed as the pannels are.

SECT. 8.

Fig. 9. The common fhutter, a fhutter which is made of mahogany, in a neat manner, with fmall pannels, and a fmall glafs window in the upper middle one: the neateft has a fmall moulding on the edge of the framings: they all have a lace tape in the middle, and a loop at the top to pull them up by.

SECT. 9.

Fig. 10. The feat-box, a box made to flide under the feat, which fills that vacant place. It is portable, and convenient to carry linen, &c. and is moftly made of thin oak or mahogany.

SECT. 10.

Fig. 11. The driving-box; a box made for the driver to fit on, fitted to the half top of the feat of a chaife, &c. for the cufhion to be placed on. It is made as the other is, and convenient for the fame purpofes.

SECT. 11.

FALSE linings, are linen linings ufed to cover and preferve the others if good, or to hide them if bad: they are made of the linen ufually called yard-wide, and at about 2s. 3d. per yard in value. The roofs are feldom covered, and as much of the trimmings as poffible fhould be fhewn.

To bind the edges of the linen lining with a border in imitation of lace, is an additional ornament to it, and is now frequently done.

All those articles may be confidered as appendages to the infide of carriages; and their value being feparately ftated, will enable any perfon to regulate the different modes of furnifhing any defcription thereof.

QUANTITY OF MATERIALS USED FOR LININGS.

THE variety of bodies, and the different methods of trimming them with lace, and furnifhing them with other conveniencies, require them to be feparately ftated; and that the different prices may be more eafily collected, the quantities of cloth and lace ufed for each kind of plain trimming fhould alfo be given, previous to the prices being ftated, fo that from one ftatement the value of all the others may be known, by adding fuch things as may be wanted out of the common way.

		YARDS.			
		Laces.		Cloth.	
		Narrow feaming.	Broad binding.	Broadcloths.	Linen.
As Fig. 2 and 3	A coach or landau	78	22	10½	18
	A chariot or demi-landau	54	18	8	14
	A phaeton or chaife	18	6	2½	5
Wings to chaife or phaeton		—	4	½	1
Head to ditto		—	—	3	6

PRICE

PRICE OF LININGS.

THE following are the prices of the various linings complete, after having been stuffed up and prepared, as before mentioned in the first statement of bodies, so that the price of new lining an old carriage is the same as that stated for a new one.

	Coach.			Chariot.			Chaise or Phaeton.* With head.			With wings.		
	£.	s.	d.	£.	s.	d.	£.	s.	d.	£.	s.	d.
The body, lined with second cloth, and trimmed with a two-inch worsted lace, and two inches and a half for holders	15	10	0	0	12	0	7	15	0	5	10	0
EXTRAS to be added to the above description.												
The body, if made to open Indian fashion	1	11	6	1	1	0	—			—		
The cloth, if superfine, instead of second	0	8	0	0	3	6	0	2	0	0	1	0
If Morocco leather, instead of cloth	1	1	0	0	10	0	0	4	0	0	2	0
The side of the lining quilted	1	1	0	0	18	0	0	6	0	0	6	0
Swing-holders, and the other laces, 2½ inch broad	1	11	6	0	18	0	0	2	0	0	3	6
Ditto ditto 3 ditto	2	7	0	1	2	0	0	5	0	—		
Ditto ditto 3¼ ditto	3	3	0	1	18	0	0	7	0	0	10	6
Ditto ditto 4 ditto	3	18	0	2	3	0	0	10	0	0	14	0
A false lining to cover the other, except the roof	3	10	0	2	15	0	0	6	0	0	7	6
Ditto, with the roof covered	4	0	0	3	3	0	0	10	0	—		
Ditto, with 2½ inch bordering to imitate lace trimmings	5	5	0	4	10	0	0	14	0	0	8	0

* These prices only include the lining, without the wood or leather work of the head.

PRICE OF INSIDE FURNITURE.

	Coach.			Chariot.		
	£.	s.	d.	£.	s.	d.
A set of silk squabs, with half backs, faced on one side with silk only	4	0	0	2	12	6
Ditto with Morocco leather	4	15	0	3	3	0
Ditto faced with silk and leather	5	15	6	3	13	6
A net for the roof, either flat or round string	0	10	6	0	10	6
A set of silk spring curtains	3	3	0	3	0	0
A set of festoon curtains, tops only	2	12	6	2	12	6
A set of ditto with side drapery	3	13	6	3	13	6
A set of glasses and glass frames, covered with cloth, the size of the glass usually about 20 inches square	6	10	0	6	15	0
Ditto covered with lace two inches wide	7	7	0	7	10	0
A set of Venetian blinds	4	10	0	4	10	0
A set of mahogany shutters	1	15	0	1	15	0

	Phaeton or Chaise.			Coach.			Chariot.		
	£.	s.	d.	£.	s.	d.	£.	s.	d.
A carpet or oil-cloth for the bottom	0	7	6	0	10	6	0	10	6
Trunks to slide under the seat	0	15	0	1	10	0	0	15	0

CHAP.

CHAP. X.

HAMMERCLOTHS.

HAMMERCLOTHS are among the principal ornaments to a carriage; they are a cloth covering to the coachman's feat, made to various patterns agreeable to the occupier's fancy. The fullnefs of the plaiting of the cloth, its depth, and the quantity of trimmings thereon, proportion the expence to almoſt any amount; but thofe of the general fort are made of a livery or fecond cloth, of fix breadths, which meafures nine yards round, and about twenty-eight inches deep, lined with a ftrong coarfe linen; the fize of the feat in a great meafure regulates the number of breadths of cloth to be ufed; as the fame fullnefs would appear with five breadths on a feat of three yards round, as fix breadths on a feat of four yards, which is the general fize now in ufe; and no hammercloth ought to be made with lefs. The top rows of fringe and lace are put on after the hammercloth is made up, and takes no more in quantity than what the feat meafures; the others extend round the fullnefs of the cloth.

SECT. 1.

OIL-SKIN HAMMERCLOTHS.

OIL-skin hammercloths are used for the preservation of the others in wet weather; there are three sorts of them, viz. the common oiled linen, the painted linen, and the painted prepared woollen or patent cloth.

The plain oil-skin, though called a skin, is only a thin linen prepared or dressed with oil, and of a very slender texture, owing to the effect the oil has upon it, which it soon rots.

The painted linen is an imitation only of the patent woollen, prepared with colours to resemble them; but are little superior to the common sort, yet are often imposed in their stead, though of not one half their value in expence or service.

The patent woollen is prepared in some secret way on a thin woollen cloth, that, for durability, exceed the service of two of the others, but is also considerably greater in expence: they are painted of various patterns, to suit most colours that the carriage is painted of. The tops of these are always made with a ridge on each side of the coachman's sitting place, which makes a channel to convey the wet from running under
him,

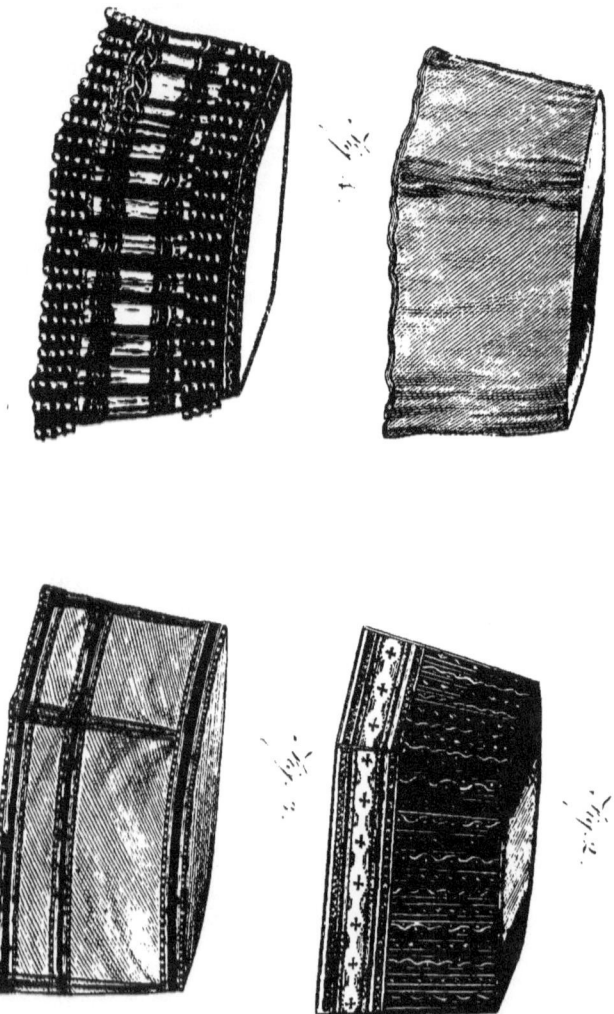

him, and have alfo thin boards placed up the four corners, to preferve their fhape.

SECT. 2.

PLATE XVI.

Fig. 1. A plain hammercloth, bound at top and bottom, with a narrow binding lace two inches wide; this reprefents alfo a plain oiled linen cover of the common fort.

Fig. 2. Reprefents the patent woollen and the painted linen covers, which fo nearly refemble each other, that the difference can only be difcovered on a near examination; the fquare place on the top is the fitting place for the coachman, which is made of woollen cloth

Fig. 3. A plain-trimmed hammercloth; the cloth of two colours, trimmed with three rows of lace two inches and a half wide: this is the kind of hammercloth generally ufed as a cover, made of four breadths, and only plaited at the corners; but, if full plaited, the quantity is as ufual.

Fig. 4. A fuller trimmed hammercloth, having three rows of lace two inches and a half wide, and two of ornamented fringe five inches deep.

PLATE XVII.

Fig. 5. A full-trimmed hammercloth, with lace three inches wide, having four rows of lace, and three of ornamented fringe, so as almost wholly to cover the cloth with the trimmings.

Fig. 6. The present fashion of hammercloths, the trimmings of which are broad, and placed on the bottom only; the lace in the middle is four, and the fringe nine inches deep; a plainer lace is at the top and bottom, two and a half inches broad for the binding; the cloth is of two colours to match the livery; the crests and mantlings are embroidered on the ends.

Fig. 7. A handsome hammercloth, trimmed with a row of two and a half inch lace at the top and bottom, and a broad four inch lace in the middle; two rows of nine-inch fringe, and silk drapery on each fringe.

Fig. 8. A hammercloth bound, top and bottom with a lace two and a half inches broad: a row of velvet is placed above the fringe, bound with a narrow lace; also a row of velvet Vandyked at the top, bound the same way, and a deep nine-inch fringe at the bottom, with silk ornaments; the arms, crest, and ornament foliage mantles are worked in embroidery on the ends.

Fig.

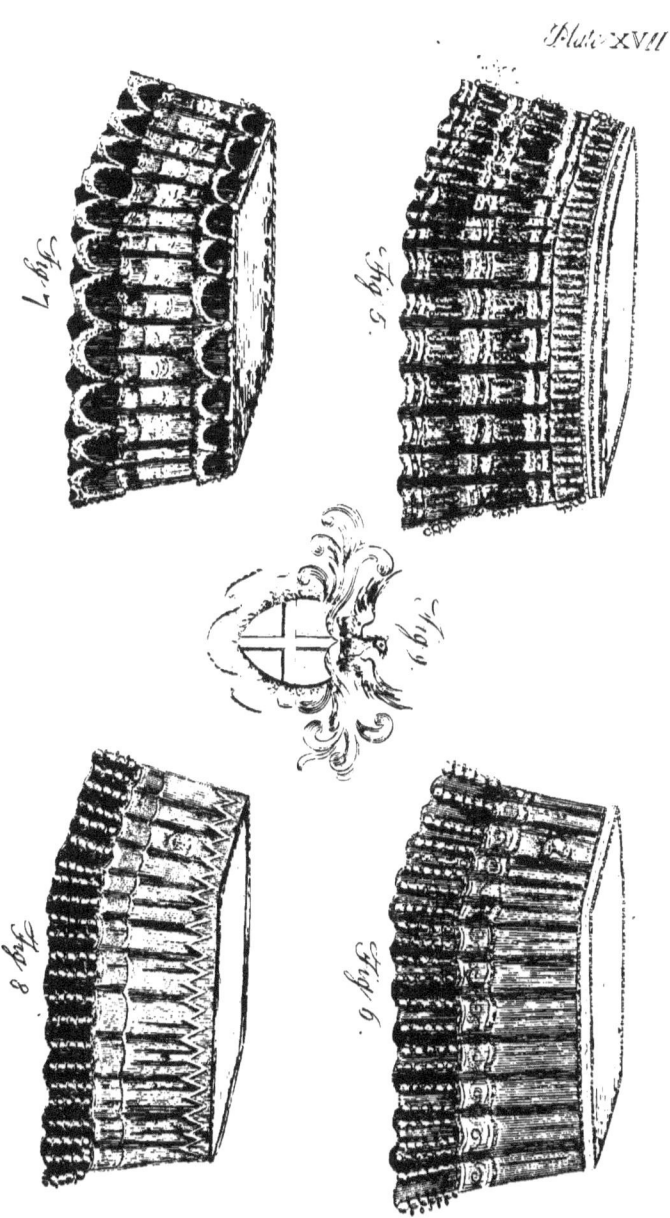

Fig. 9. Reprefents the embroidery now ufually worn upon hammercloths, which is done in various fanciful devices, the principal of which are the arms, crefts, and cyphers, worked on the ground plain, or in mantles of the curtain or foliage patterns. They are moftly worked in worfted and filk, and the feparate prices are ftated with thofe of hammercloths.

PRICE OF HAMMERCLOTHS.

TO obtain correct information of the value of any fort of hammercloths, it is neceffary to know the quantity of cloth and trimmings they are made up with, which depends on the fize of the feat: it meafuring in common four yards round, requires nine yards to plait round it, with a proper fullnefs, which is fix breadths of 6-quarter broad-cloth, cut in lengths of 7-8ths or 3-4ths of a yard, and fewed together; fo that a fix-breadth hammer-cloth, which is the ufual fize, takes nine yards of each trimming to go round the cloth, and four yards for the top; fo that to add or reduce a breadth, is to allow one-fixth from the following ftatements, or one yard and a half of each trimming, and 7-8ths of a yard of cloth, for every breadth added or omitted.

The

PRICE OF HAMMERCLOTHS.

The patterns of hammercloths described in Plates xvi. and xvii. being what are generally used, the separate prices are here stated, according as they are described, to convey a ready information of collecting the amount of any other, by referring to the former statements.

	Livery.	Second.	Superfine.
	£. s. d.	£. s. d.	£. s. d.
A hammercloth made up of six breadths, containing 5¼ yards of broad-cloth, without trimmings — —	4 10 0	5 10 0	6 10 0
Ditto, with the following trimmings, of livery cloth:			
13 yds. of 2-inch lace — as Fig. 1.	5 5 0		
22 yds. of 2½ inch lace — Fig. 3.	6 6 0		
22 yds. of 2¼ inch lace, and 9 yds. of 5-inch ornamented fringe — Fig. 4.	9 9 0		
31 yds. of 3-inch lace, and 22 yds. of 6-inch ornamented fringe — Fig. 5.	17 0 0		
13 yds. of 2½ inch lace, 9 yds. of 4-inch lace, and 9 yds. of 9-inch ornamented fringe, worsted crest and mantling on the ends Fig. 6.	14 0 0		
13 yds. of 2½ inch lace, 9 yds. of 4-inch lace, and 13 yds. of 7-inch fringe, two rows of silk drapery — Fig. 7.	18 12 0		
13 yds. of 2¼ inch lace, 9 yds. of 8-inch plain fringe, 13 yds. of 4-inch velvet at 4s. and 36 yds of 1-inch binding at 1s. silk crest and mantling on the ends — Fig. 8.	14 7 0		

		Worsted and Silk.
EMBROIDERY.		
Crest or cyphers only — —		1 5 0
Crests and mantles only — —		2 0 0
Arms and crests — —		2 10 0
Arms, crests, and mantles — —		3 3 0

For other cloths add the difference of price as above.

CHAP

CHAP. XI.

PLATED, BRASS, AND COMPOSITION METAL FURNITURE FOR BODIES, &c.

SECT. 1.

THE neceffary conveniencies and ornaments for the bodies being of various defcriptions, and as varioufly finifhed, it is neceffary to introduce them feparately, that the variety may be the better underftood : fome of them form a part of the original bodies, which being articles neceffary to build with, their value is included in the former ftatement of Bodies, and are only here introduced for a general defcription of their form: fome of the other articles have alfo been formerly reprefented in the fubject of iron-work; but being what are frequently plated, they are here defcribed under that head, and the increafed amount, for plating only, is added : there are fome which are only occafionally ufed, and others that are different in their form from each

other,

other, which makes it neceffary to treat of them feparate from the bodies, that their different values may be known, and their advantages the better underftood, as reprefented in Plate xviii.

DOOR PLATES.

Fig. 1. The door-plates, which are made of brafs, are fixed round the edges of the door with fcrews, having, in the folid brafs, a bead or moulding which forms two rabbets; the one laps on, and confines, the door-pannel, the other covers the joint when the door is fhut.

DOOR HINGES.

Fig. 2, Are ftrong hinges of a peculiar form, made either of brafs or iron, having a ridge on the outfide, to ftop the door from turning too far back in the opening.

DOOR LOCKS AND HANDLES.

Fig. 3. A door box-lock, which is a flat fquare box brazed on a flat iron plate, having within the box a broad flat tongue or bolt, which is turned by a fquare fpindle fixed through it, on the end of which fpindle the handle A is hung, by which the bolt is turned: the form of the handle fhould be made agreeable to the pattern of the buckles ufed for the braces, whether round, fquare, oval, or octagon. Thofe box-locks are morticed in the door pillars, and fixed by the plate to which they are brazed: a flat plate, with a fquare hole, is funk in the oppofite pillar over the mortice which receives the tongue. The handles are moftly plated, and the price is included in the former ftatements of bodies.

PRIVATE LOCKS.

Fig. 4. Are box-locks, made in the fame form and fixed in the ftanding pillars the fame way as the others are in the door-pillars; they are fometimes made with wards, and a bolt, the fame as common locks, and are turned with a common key,

key, but are moſt frequently made as the door-locks, to turn with a pipe-key; the key-hole is covered with a double ſcutcheon.

DOVE-TAILED KETCHES.

Fig. 5. Are two ſmall iron machines, which fit cloſely in a dove-tailed joint within each other, and are ſeparately fixed on the ſhutting door and ſtanding pillar; their uſe is to prevent the door from dropping or ſinking by its weight.

GLASS ROLLERS.

Fig. 6 and 7. Theſe belong to the inſide work of a body, for the affiſtance of drawing up the glaſſes with; they are made of ſeveral patterns, from three to four inches long, of braſs, and are only plated with a thin leaf of ſilver; as they do not require to be cleaned like the outſide plating, they anſwer the purpoſe ſufficiently well; the ſunk rollers are at preſent moſt in uſe, and are the beſt, being more out of the way.

BUTTONS

BUTTONS OR STUDS.

Fig. 8. Thefe are nails with large brafs heads; if ufed to the infide of bodies, are then filvered; but if ufed for outfide purpofes, fuch as for knee-boots, they fhould be plated, but are feldom fo done.

MOST of thofe articles are what is neceffary for building the body with, and are included in the value of bodies in the former ftatements: what are only occafionally ufed, and fhould be charged extra for, will here be ftated.

PRICE OF OCCASIONAL REQUISITES.

	£.	s.	d.
A pair of private locks and bolts to the fhutters, complete, for coach or chariot	1	1	0
A fet of filvered glafs rollers, four inches long	0	10	6
A fingle filvered knee-boot button	0	0	4
Ditto, if plated	0	8	0

SECT. 2.

PLATING.

PLATING is a fuperficial covering to the buckles and other furniture of a carriage, either with filver or metal of any other malleable quality. Nothing has ever been introduced with a better effect than this mode of ornament; in particular, the filver plating, which is now become fo general, that almoft every hackney carriage exhibits fome portion of it.

There is no one article in the carriage can be of a more deceitful quality, as it can be manufactured at almoft any price, even cheaper than the original brafs ornaments, and yet look well; in particular the flat plates and beaded mouldings, being manufactured with different proportions of filver foldered on to a certain quantity of metal, which, after being thus plated, is rolled or flatted in mills to any degree of thinnefs, leaving fometimes but barely the colour of the filver, which is frequently not thicker than a common leaf of beaten filver. Other filver plated articles, which are wrought by hand, fuch as buckles, handles, terrets, &c. are plated in a different way, and cannot be done but with fome degree of thicknefs; the thinneft of which will wear some confiderable time longer than the common rolled filver plating. The difference of light and ftrong plating is an object worth attending to, as there is more than double the odds of price between the two extremes, particularly in the beads or flat ornaments. A dependence muft here be placed on the manufacturer for the quality, as the appearance is fo exact, that, unlefs analyfed, no other perfon can tell the proportion they bear. The patterns of the furniture are numerous; thofe are the beft calculated for wear that have no raifed or fharp edges; the round-moulded furniture has the faireft chance, and is, for the moft part, the cheapeft; all ornaments that are raifed, fuch as fcrolls, crefts, &c. fhould be of filver, as the cleaning foon fpoils them, if only plated.

It is next to impoffible to enumerate every article that is fometimes plated; what is moft generally ufed will only be defcribed: there are a number of plated articles ufed to harnefs, which will not here be noticed, but will be in the fecond volume, under the defcription of harnefs; all that will be here defcribed is the furniture for the carriage, which principally lies in the mouldings, head-plates, joints, &c.

SECT. 3.

BRASS AND COLOURED METAL FURNITURE.

THE furniture and ornaments to a carriage were originally made of brafs; and, now that filver plating has become fo common, brafs is again become more fafhionable, but improved from the original manner of making it: the common brafs furniture is ufually made out of the folid metal, fuch as the mouldings, head-plates, buckles, and rings; but the other furniture where the ftrength of iron is neceffary, fuch as the joints, is plated with brafs, in the fame manner as when plated with filver. There is alfo a metal ufed, which is a compofition of brafs and copper, which looks well, and is more malleable than brafs for plating with; the principal objection to thofe metals is, that they foon tarnifh and canker, and are much more difficult to clean than filver plating.

The price for filver plating being fo much reduced, makes the difference between it and brafs furniture not fo great as many people imagine. To take it in general, the common brafs furniture is about one half, and the compofition is about two-thirds of the price of the beft plated filver.

SECT. 4.

THE MOULDINGS OR BEADS.

MOULDINGS are of various patterns and fizes, and of as many different qualities; but to reduce the variety to a few rules, will furnifh fufficient information. The infide cavities are filled with a folder which holds the fhanks for the mouldings to be faftened on with. The quality of the filver plating fhould be fuch, that in the conftant ufe of a carriage, with proper cleaning, it fhall remain perfect four years, and feven without wearing through, except at the edges. The middling fort fhould wear two years perfect, and three without wearing through, except at the edges. On the inferior fort there can be no dependence whatever. Brafs and compofition metal mouldings, not being plated, but made of the folid metal, can never be injured by wear. The width of the mouldings proportions the value; it is meafured acrofs the bottom, and fold by the foot, including the putting on. The patterns make no material difference in the expence, as they are all drawn through a mould to any form; the difference in the trouble is only in the fetting and burnifhing; therefore, to proportion the

prices

prices to a certain width and quality, will anfwer every purpofe of information.

Fig. 8. Is the fmall quill bead, moftly put on in double rows, which has a very neat appearance.

Fig. 9. Is the general fort of moulding in ufe, which looks bold, and wears well.

Fig. 10. Is a neat pattern moulding, made hollow in the middle, and rounding on the fides, and, having no fharp edges, wears well.

Fig. 11. The common flat moulding, much ufed: the edges of this moulding are foon rubbed through by cleaning.

Fig. 12. A fancy moulding, feldom ufed but to handfome carriages, and is moftly made of a double angle to clip the corner: the many edges to this moulding require to be ftrongly plated, to wear well.

Fig. 13. A very common pattern moulding, which looks rich, but, on account of the raifed edges, does not wear well.

Fig. 14. A fcroll and tip ornament, made to give a finifhed appearance to where the bead terminates at the ends of the bottom, fides, &c. Thefe ornaments fhould always be made of thin filver.

PRICE OF MOULDINGS.

FIG. 8, 9, 10, 11, 12, 13.

Size.	Best.		Silver Plated. Middling.		Inferior.		Composition Metal.		Brass.	
Inch.	s.	d.	s.	d.	s.	d.	s.	d.	s.	d.
2-8ths	1	3	1	0	0	9	0	10	0	8
3-8ths	1	9	1	6	1	0	1	2	0	10½
4-8ths	2	3	1	9	1	3	1	6	1	1½
5-8ths	2	9	2	3	1	6	1	10	1	4½
6-8ths	3	3	2	9	1	9	2	2	1	9½

SCROLL AND TIP ORNAMENTS.

FIG. 14.

	Silver.		Best plated Metal.		Composition Metal.		Brass.	
	s.	d.	s.	d.	s.	d.	s.	d.
A pair of scroll ornaments	8	0	6	4	4	0	3	0
A pair of tip ornaments	6	0	4	0	2	8	2	0

SECT. 5.

FRAMES.

FOR many part of the bodies the mouldings are obliged to be made into frames, by first setting them to the form intended, and then solder-
ing

170   PLATED, BRASS, AND COMPOSITION

ing the joints previous to putting them on, for which an extraordinary charge for each joint, and for each fet, is to be allowed, in addition to the quantity of moulding ufed ; and an inch over the exact meafure for jointing; but, unlefs foldered at the joints, ought only to be charged with the other mouldings, allowing for each fet only.

Fig. 15. A plated wing-frame, is a broad cafed moulding, with which the wing-frame is covered : befides allowing for the width and meafure, five fhillings each for putting them on fhould be added; the pattern in general runs large, and is about 3 feet 6 inches in length each frame.

Fig. 16. An octagon frame, formed to the back light or window, put on previous to the glafs being fixed.

Fig. 17. A whole fword-cafe frame ; a moulding bent in the form of the fword-cafe end, and fixed thereon.

Fig. 18. A half fword-cafe frame ; a moulding formed to the outer fhape only of the fword-cafe end.

Fig. 19. A fham or real door-frame; a moulding fhaped to the pattern of the contracted part of the fide of a chaife or phaeton body, called a door.

PRICE

METAL FURNITURE FOR BODIES.

PRICE OF FRAMES.

	Silver Plated.			Composition Metal.	Brass.
	Best. £. s. d.	Middling £. s. d.	Inferior. £. s. d.	£. s. d.	£. s. d.
An octagon or back-light frame	0 10 0	0 9 0	0 8 0	0 7 8	0 5 0
A pair of sword-case frames	0 11 0	0 10 0	0 9 0	0 8 4	0 5 6
A pair of half ditto	0 11 0	0 1 0	0 1 0	0 5 4	0 4 0
A pair of wing frames	1 15 0	1 10 0	1 1 0	1 4 0	0 18 0

SECT. 6.

HEAD PLATES.

THESE are ornaments made to fix on the upper quarters of a coach or chariot, and on the flats of a chaise head; they are of various patterns, and of different qualities of metal; but should be in proportion to the beadings with which the body is plated: they are made of a fancy device, or are left open for the crest to be placed within; the patterns, except with crests, make no material difference in the price; the size and quality make the only difference worth notice.

Fig.

PLATED, BRASS, AND COMPOSITION

Fig. 20. A fancy-worked head-plate, the middle and bottom ornamented with chafing and piercing.

Fig. 21. A fashionable bead-rim head-plate for a creſt to go in, ſometimes ornamented with a bottom huſk the ſame as the other.

Fig. 22. A creſt which is ſometimes made large, and wore alone, but moſtly is made of a ſize to be placed within the circle: of theſe there are different ſorts; ſome are pierced out of flat metal, and a little raiſed from the back, in imitation of emboſſed work; others are properly emboſſed: the circles, if raiſed, ſhould alſo be made of thin ſilver; the difference of expence is but trifling compared with the advantage.

PRICE

METAL FURNITURE FOR BODIES.

PRICE OF HEAD PLATES, PER SET.

FIG. 20, 21, 22.

Number of Head Plates to a Coach 12, Chariot 6, Phaeton 9.

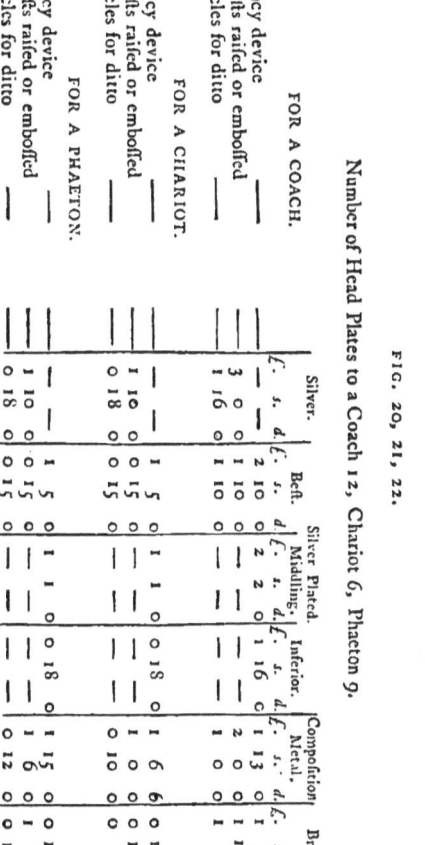

	Silver			Best			Silver Plated. Middling.			Inferior.			Composition Metal.			Brass.		
	£	s.	d.	£	s.	d.	£	s.	d.	£	s.	d.	£	s.	d.	£	s.	d.
FOR A COACH.																		
Fancy device	3	0	0	2	10	0	—	—	—	—	—	—	2	0	0	1	5	0
Crests raised or embossed	1	16	0	1	10	0	2	2	0	1	16	0	1	13	0	1	5	0
Circles for ditto	—	—	—	1	15	0	—	—	—	—	—	—	1	0	0	—	—	—
FOR A CHARIOT.																		
Fancy device	—	—	—	—	—	—	—	—	—	—	—	—	1	0	6	0	12	6
Crests raised or embossed	0	18	0	0	15	0	1	5	0	0	18	0	1	0	6	0	15	0
Circles for ditto	—	—	—	0	15	0	—	—	—	—	—	—	0	10	0	0	7	6
FOR A PHAETON.																		
Fancy device	—	—	—	—	—	—	—	—	—	—	—	—	0	15	6	0	10	0
Crests raised or embossed	1	10	0	0	15	0	1	0	0	0	18	0	0	12	0	0	10	0
Circles for ditto	—	—	—	0	15	0	—	—	—	—	—	—	0	10	0	—	—	—

SECT. 7.

REAL AND SHAM JOINTS.

FIG. 23, 24, 25.

PLATED joints give to the body a very bold rich appearance, for which reason they are frequently used to bodies with fixed heads, but then are only for ornament, in imitation of the real joints: there is a material difference in the value of them; the real joint is obliged to be plated both on the out and inside on the eight squares; the sham joint is made thin and broad, and plated only on the outside on the three squares, which are made broader than the others, for show: others are made thick and heavy, in exact imitation of the real joint, and plated on the five squares; those are all plated with silver foldered on the iron, the thinnest of which will wear equal to the best moulding, and what is bestowed on them, more than will sufficiently wear with the other furniture, is superfluous; the nut-screws, by which the sham or real joints are fixed, are plated; and sometimes the props, on which the joints are supported from the sides, are also plated, and have a broad, flat cap, plated, and put thereon: chaise joints are charged in sets, landau joints only in pairs.

METAL FURNITURE FOR BODIES.

Chaife head and landau joints, painted black, are included in the value with the head of the chaife and the body of the landau. The additional expence for plating is only to be added here; fham joints are never ufed otherwife than plated, and their value, with putting on, &c. is here ftated in full.

PRICE OF REAL AND SHAM JOINTS.

	Silver Plated.			Compofition Metal.			Brafs.		
	£.	s.	d.	£.	s.	d.	£.	s.	d.
A fet for a landau	12	12	0	8	8	0	6	6	0
A fet for a chair or curricle	8	0	0	5	5	0	4	4	0
A pair for a landaulet	6	6	0	4	4	0	3	3	0
A fet of thick fham joints for a coach	7	0	0	4	12	0	3	10	0
A fet of thin light ditto, ditto	6	0	0	4	0	0	3	0	0
A pair of thick fham joints for a chariot	3	10	0	2	6	6	1	3	0
A pair of thin light ditto, ditto	3	0	0	2	0	0	1	15	0
Four barrel props and caps for a pair of either	1	4	0	0	18	0	0	12	0

SECT. 8.

BODY LOOPS.

Fig. 26. Thofe are plated in the fame manner as the joints, but generally only in particular places,

places, from the neck to the loop, either on the small outside edges, the star, or the flat bolt-heads; sometimes the whole surface from the neck to the loop is plated; the value of the loop having been before included with the body, the price here stated is only for the extra amount of plating.

PRICE OF BODY LOOPS, PER PAIR.

	Silver Plated.			Composition Metal.			Brass.		
	£.	s.	d.	£.	s.	d.	£.	s.	d.
Plating the whole surface from the neck	3	13	6	2	6	0	1	12	0
Ditto the four star heads	0	10	0	0	6	6	0	5	0
Ditto the four plain heads	0	8	0	0	5	4	0	4	0
Ditto the two top outer edges	0	6	0	0	4	0	0	3	0

SECT. 9.

POLE HOOK.

Fig. 27. This is a convenience for drawing by, but is frequently put on the end of the pole for ornament only: it is plated, the same as the others, upon iron, sometimes is only painted, but more frequently used plated than otherwise: the value of each is here stated, including the buckle and

METAL FURNITURE FOR BODIES.

and strap, and fixing on the pole; there are three sizes of them in general use.

PRICE OF POLE HOOKS.

	Plain Iron.			Silver Plated.			Composition Metal.			Brass.		
	£.	s.	d.	£.	s.	d.	£.	s.	d.	£.	s.	d.
Large size for a coach	0	10	0	2	10	0	1	15	0	1	6	0
Middle ditto, for a chariot —	0	9	0	2	2	0	1	8	0	1	1	0
Small ditto, for a phaeton —	0	8	0	1	18	0	0	18	6	0	15	0

SECT. 10.

BUCKLES.

Fig. 28. The plated buckles used to a carriage are few, but large, and are plated, like the rest, on iron; the main-brace buckles are the principal, those besides are for the check braces; the pole-piece buckles are sometimes plated, but in general are only polished iron; the value of all buckles are regulated by their size as follows:

PLATED, BRASS, AND COMPOSITION

PRICE OF BUCKLES, PER PAIR.

		Silver Plated.			Composition Metal.			Brass.		
		£.	s.	d.	£.	s.	d.	£.	s.	d.
Half buckles	2¾	0	7	0	0	4	6	0	3	6
	2½	0	6	0	0	4	0	0	3	0
	2¼	0	5	0	0	3	0	0	2	6
	2	0	4	0						
	1¾	0	3	0	0	2	0	0	1	6
	1½	0	2	0	0	1	4	0	1	0
Whole buckles	2¾	0	11	0	0	7	0	0	5	6
	2½	0	9	0	0	6	0	0	4	6
	2¼	0	7	6	0	5	0	0	3	9
	2	0	6	0	0	4	0	0	3	0
	1¾	0	4	0	0	3	6	0	2	6
	1½	0	3	0	0	2	6	0	2	0

SECT. 11.

CHECK-BRACE RINGS AND DOOR HANDLES.

Fig. 29 and 30. Thofe fcrew-rings and door-handles are always plated like the reft of the iron-work; the price for plating the rings is to be added to the former ftatements of bodies; but as, on many occafions, they are required feparate, it will be neceffary to price them both plain and plated. Plated handles are included in the former ftatements.

PRICE

PRICE OF CHECK-BRACE RINGS AND DOOR HANDLES, PER PAIR.

	Plain Iron.			Silver Plated.			Composition Metal.			Brass.		
	£	s	d	£	s	d	£	s	d	£	s	d
Check-brace rings	0	2	0	0	8	0	0	5	6	0	4	0
Door handles	0	3	0	0	12	0	0	8	0	0	6	0

SECT. 12.

WHEEL HOOPS.

Fig. 31. It is very common to plate the hoops of the wheels both at the back and fore end of the nave. The fore hoop is confiderably broader than the hind one; but the circumference being lefs, its value is nearly equal. They are great ornaments to the carriage, and, with care, will laft two or three fets of wheels, according as they are plated. There are two methods of plating hoops, the one to plate with filver on the iron, the fame as thefe laft articles, but generally are only cafed with the rolled plated metal; they may be reckoned of three fizes, large for coach, middle for chariot, and fmall for phaeton or chaife.

PRICE OF WHEEL HOOPS, PER PAIR.

		Coach.			Chariot.			Phaeton or Chaise.		
		£.	s.	d.	£.	s.	d.	£.	s.	d.
Plated with silver on iron	—	3	3	0	2	12	6	2	2	0
Cased with plated metal { best		1	15	0	1	10	0	1	5	0
mid.		1	10	0	1	5	0	1	0	0
infer.		1	5	0	1	1	0	0	15	0
Composition	—	2	2	0	1	11	0	1	8	0
Brass	—	1	11	6	1	7	0	1	1	0

CHAP.

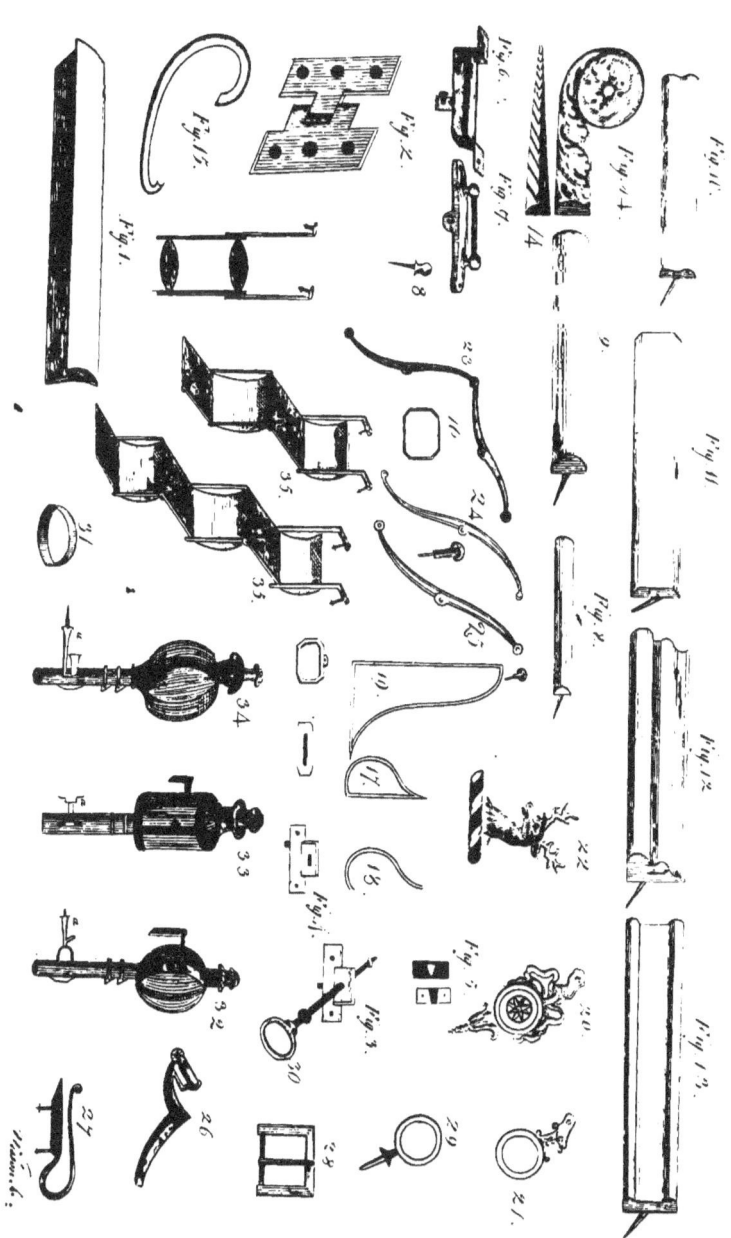

CHAP. XII.

LAMPS.

PLATE XVIII.

LAMPS were originally ufed as neceffary conveniencies to a carriage, but are now principally ufed for ornament, for which they are as well calculated as any article throughout. They are of various patterns, and are diftinguifhed by the name of the globe, the Italian, or oval lamp: the oval lamp is now the moft general in ufe, and, like the globe, it cafts the light entirely forward: the Italian lamp does not reflect fo ftrong a light forward, but gives a light all round them, which is convenient to paffengers in the carriage. There have been fome few lamps ufed of the patent principle for burning oil, but the fmoke they create renders their ufe objectionable; the hard fpermaceti candle is the beft to burn. The lamps are frequently fmothered, or the lights go out, for want of fufficient openings at the bottom and top to receive the air, and to difcharge the fmoke; the lamps are of three kinds,

kinds, three sizes, and are three ways finished, either plain or ornamented, with plating or glafs reflectors; the large size is used to the coach; the middle size to the chariot; the small to the gig or phaeton: they are fixed by iron-work, differently formed, according as the lamps are required to be set; the barrels are supported by small iron forks or props, and are made secure with a leather strap and buckle. The following reprefent the three lamps now moftly in ufe, which are called the globe, the Italian, and the oval pattern lamps.

Fig. 32. The globe lamp, made round in the body, and has one large concave glafs in front.

Fig. 33. The Italian lamp, made long, but round in the body, and has the glafs in three divifions.

Fig. 34. The oval lamp, has a glafs in front, a little convexed, and two bent fmall glaffes on the fides.

Thefe lamps are all manufactured of tin, on one principle, with a long cafe or barrel for the candle, having in the barrel a fpiral wire fpring, which raifes the candle as it confumes. The barrel is fixed in a focket of the lamp, from which it is drawn, and alfo opens at top, for the candle to be placed in, and is faftened by two
rings,

rings, or ferrels; when it is once turned round, a stop prevents it going farther: it has a small staple for the strap to be placed through, and is kept steady by forks, or props, which screw on the pillar. The heads are of various patterns, with fret, or open work, for the smoke to discharge at. The lamps remain fixed; but every time candles are used, the barrels are obliged to be taken asunder, and replaced with some trouble, and the probability of damaging or rubbing off the paint; to remedy which, the following simple plan is here submitted as an improvement, without making an increase in the expence: Let the barrel remain fixed to the lamp, and the bottom of the barrel to open on a hinge, and fasten by a spring ketch on the opposite side, and so place the candle up from the bottom, instead of taking off the barrel to put it in at the top; which is done without the least trouble or injury.

PRICE OF LAMPS.

THE plating used to lamps is of rolled plated metal, which, in general, is of the worst sort; the reason is, the prices paid to the makers for them are so low as to make it impossible to afford a sufficiently

ficiently good article; but the prices here stated allow a sufficiency for the best quality of plating; the deductions to be made for the inferior plating are, two shillings for the middling, and four shillings for the inferior sort, for each pair.

GLOBE PATTERN.

FIG. 32.

	Large.			Middle.			Small.		
	£.	s.	d.	£.	s.	d.	£.	s.	d.
A pair of plain, with common backs	1	18	0	1	15	0	1	12	0
A pair of ditto, with glass reflector backs	2	2	0	1	18	0	1	8	0
A pair with glass backs, plated heads and barrels	2	10	0	2	6	0	1	16	6

ITALIAN LAMPS.

FIG. 33.

	Large.			Middle.			Small.		
	£.	s.	d.	£.	s.	d.	£.	s.	d.
A pair of plain Italian, flat sides	1	15	0	1	12	0	1	10	0
A pair of ditto, with round sides	2	4	0	2	0	0	1	15	0
A pair of ditto, with plated heads and barrels	2	12	0	2	8	0	2	2	0

NEW PATTERN OVAL.

FIG. 34.

	Large.			Middle.			Small.		
	£.	s.	d.	£.	s.	d.	£.	s.	d.
A pair of plain ovals, but with glafs reflector backs —	2	6	0	2	2	0	1	18	0
A pair of ditto, plated —	2	10	0	2	8	0	2	6	0
A pair of ditto, with extra large plated heads — —	3	3	0	2	16	0	2	10	0

The props, ftaples, and ftraps, *a a a*, and alfo the painting, being neceffary for all lamps, the above ftatements include them.

The mounting the lamps with brafs or coloured metal, is the fame expence as mounting with filver plated metal.

REFLECTORS FOR LAMPS.

THE common reflector is only a filvered back burnifhed, which will not admit of cleaning otherwife than with a little whitening and a foft cloth tenderly ufed.

The general fort of reflector now in ufe, is a concave, thin, reflecting glafs, or looking glafs, cut in fmall diamonds or ftars, and ftuck on the back: the fmoke from thefe is eafily wiped off, and always look well.

The

The beſt and ſtrongeſt reflectors are thoſe new-invented thick convex glaſſes which are put before the light at a proper diſtance. Thoſe glaſſes anſwer beſt for the front; being of a ſtrong ſubſtance, they are not ſo eaſily broken as the others, and they magnify the light to a great advantage, but are an addition in the expence of 1l. 6s. for each pair.

CHAP.

CHAP. XIII.

STEPS.

STEPS being of various patterns, the expence both for the iron-work and trimming is alfo different, which makes it neceffary to treat of them feparately from any other fubject. Great exactnefs is required in the making them, fo that one joint may not bear a greater preffure than another, as the twift thereof would occafion it to break.

SECT. 1.

INSIDE FOLDING STEPS.

Fig. 35. The double and treble fteps ufed to clofe carriages, and hung on the bottom fides, are made convenient to fold in a fmall compafs, and adapted to the height of the body; they are lined at the back and under part of the treads with good leather, of which they take a confider-

able

able quantity; the treads are all covered with carpet the fame as the bottom of the body, and the fore fide lined and trimmed with cloth and lace the fame as the infide lining.

SECT. 2.

STEP-PLATES AND STOPS.

a. The ftep-plate, fixed in the bottom fide to preferve the timber from injury by the ftrain.

b. The ftep-ftop, which bolts on the bottom of the bottom fide, and receives the preffure of the ftep when down,

---

SECT. 3.

OUTSIDE CHAISE STEPS.

Fig. 36. The double fteps ufed, and fixed to the outfide of a body for a doctor's, or a two-wheeled carriage. They are of a fimple defign, and bear no comparifon with the other, having only one folding joint in them, being always fixed on the outfide, to prevent trouble. The treads are.

are, or ought always to be, covered with leather, to prevent accident by flipping off; their forms are various, fometimes of a bell, an oval, or fquare fhape, as fancy may direct.

SECT. 4.

HANGING STEPS.

TO high phaetons, befides the fixed treads, there are many fteps devifed, made fo as to be ufed occafionally, for the more eafy accommodation of ladies; they are moftly made to be hooked on to an upper tread when ufed; and, when out of ufe, are placed in a cafe, either at the bottom of the body, or the under part of the *carriage*.

PRICE OF STEPS.

SINGLE fteps to *carriages* compofe a part of the neceffary iron-work, and are included in the ftatements given in pages 67, 79, and 80; but as double fteps are frequently ufed to chaife or curricle *carriages*, the value of both fingle and double are here feparately ftated, that the difference may be known.

Double

STEPS.

Double and treble folding-steps for coach and chariot bodies, are only here stated, that either pattern may be added to the former statement of bodies, and save the trouble of subtracting the difference of expence of one pattern from another.

	Single.			Double.			Treble.		
	£.	s.	d.	£.	s.	d.	£.	s.	d.
A pair of inside folding-steps for coaches, &c.	—	—	—	3	10	0	5	10	0
A pair of outside steps for chaises, &c.	1	1	0	1	15	0	—	—	—
A hanging step for a phaeton -	1	1	0	2	2	0	3	3	0

The cloth and lace with which the folding-steps are trimmed, are both included in the price of linings, being a part of that article; but that the complete price of steps may be known separate, add to the above statements of inside folding steps, five shillings for the cloth and plain lace used for trimming each pair.

CHAP.

CHAP. XIV.

PAINTING, VARNISHING, &c.

PAINTING is not only neceffary to preferve, but ferves, in a great degree, to ornament the carriage, which it does more effectually than any thing elfe beftowed on it; and every attention of a proprietor ought to be, to felect fuch patterns of colours as fhall beft anfwer the purpofes of appearance and durability. The choice of colour depends entirely on fancy; but thofe fhould be preferred that are the moft permanent, or that are the leaft likely to be injured by the weather; an agreeable contraft in the colours of the body, the carriage, and ftripes, with which they are ornamented, requires fome judgment, to give a proper effect to the painting.

SECT. 1.

GROUND COLOURS.

THE ground colours are the bodies of paint with which the carriage is covered previous to varnifhing; the pannels of the body are firft prepared with a compofition laid feveral times on with a brufh, which fills the grain of the wood, and hardens fo as to bear rubbing down to a fine furface with pumice-ftone, previous to the paint being laid on; the frame-work is only covered with as many coats of paint as will fill the grain or pores of the timber. The preferable colours for wear are thofe which are extracted from minerals, fuch as the vermilion reds, yellows, whites, &c.; the moft objectionable colours are the greens, in particular the verdigrife green, though the moft agreeable colour when frefh, yet very fubject to decay. Very light colours are the leaft likely to ftand, or be well painted, as the varnifh is naturally of a darkifh hue, which is apt to ftain or cloud them; the darker the colours are, the fuller the varnifh may be laid on, and the ftronger the reflection is from it; befides, a dark colour fhews the plated furniture to the greateft advantage.

SECT. 2.

PICKING OUT.

THE picking out to a carriage is the ornamenting the ground with various contrasted colours, which is to lighten the appearance, and shew the mouldings to advantage. There are various methods of picking out, according to fancy; but the usual method is, to paint the mouldings with one full colour, different from the ground, which is called full-beading; another is to full-bead and line the sides or squares with light strokes, called lining the beads; another is to full-bead, line, and pannel, which is to paint the beads or mouldings as before, and draw fine lines along the flat surfaces of the timbers, in imitation of, and is called, pannelling, and also ornamenting with stars or scrolls in the broad spaces.

SECT. 3.

VARNISHING.

VARNISH is of material use, both for preserving the colours, and shewing them to advantage, and may be so executed as to reflect

reflect like a mirror; it is made of diffolved gums in oil and fpirits, and with it the painting is covered. The durability of the varnifh depends much on care; but frequently fails, in confequence of being too new when ufed, or made of an inferior compofition; the higher the varnifh is on the pannels, the better they look, but are the lefs likely to ftand: the dark varnifh in general has the ftrongeft body, but cannot be ufed to cover light painting, as it fo much difcolours it; the light varnifh is in general fo thin as fcarcely to fhew any luftre, without a confiderable quantity, which is difficult to lay on without clouding; fome varnifh, foon after ufe, lofes its luftre, and looks as dull as if no varnifh at all had been ufed; others crack all over, but principally on thofe parts which are moft expofed to the fun; this circumftance is owing to the compofition; that is, whether the gums, oils, or fpirits, moft preponderate; on the quality of the varnifh the permanency of the paint principally depends.

There are three methods of varnifhing the pannels, viz. the common, the polifhed, and high varnifh; the common varnifhing is what is done to all, and is included in the charge of painting; the polifhed is an additional quantity of three or four coats of varnifh extra, which, after being properly hardened, is fmoothed and polifhed with fine powder and hard rubbing; the

high

high varnish is a still greater number of coats of the best varnish, which is polished so as to give it a very high lustre, almost equal to a looking-glass.

SECT. 4.

JAPANNING.

THE japanning is covering the leathered or upper parts of the body and boots, &c. of a carriage, with a fine black, in the manner of painting; it is a composition of gums, spirits, and spaltams, of a thin body, resembling varnish; it is a strong contrast to the other colours, and answers both for colour and varnish, and may be polished equal to it.

SECT. 5.

HERALD AND ORNAMENT PAINTING.

IT is usual, for the distinction of families, to paint on the pannels the arms and crests they are entitled to bear, from the Office of Heraldry.

The arms of private families are borne in plain fhields, but thofe of the nobility have fupporters and coronets of various patterns. A minute defcription of the rules of Herald Painting would be unneceffary here; a reference to *Edmonfon's Book of Heraldry* will give every information on that fubject. Plate xix. and the defcription thereof, will give fuch information as is commonly required.

The ornament painting is merely to beautify the carriage, which it does materially, when it is well executed; but, when otherwife, it hurts the appearance of it. This depends on the capacity of the artift : the pannels had better be entirely plain, than daubed, as many of them are, in imitation of painting; and in particular that of Heraldry, which requires fome merit to execute it properly.

PLATE XIX.

Fig. 1. The arms of a bachelor in fhield, with the creft on a wreath.

Fig. 2. The arms of a maiden lady, in the proper-fhaped lozenge they fhould be borne.

Fig. 3. The arms of the fame, empalled with thofe of the gentleman's, fhewing how they are borne when united by marriage.

Fig.

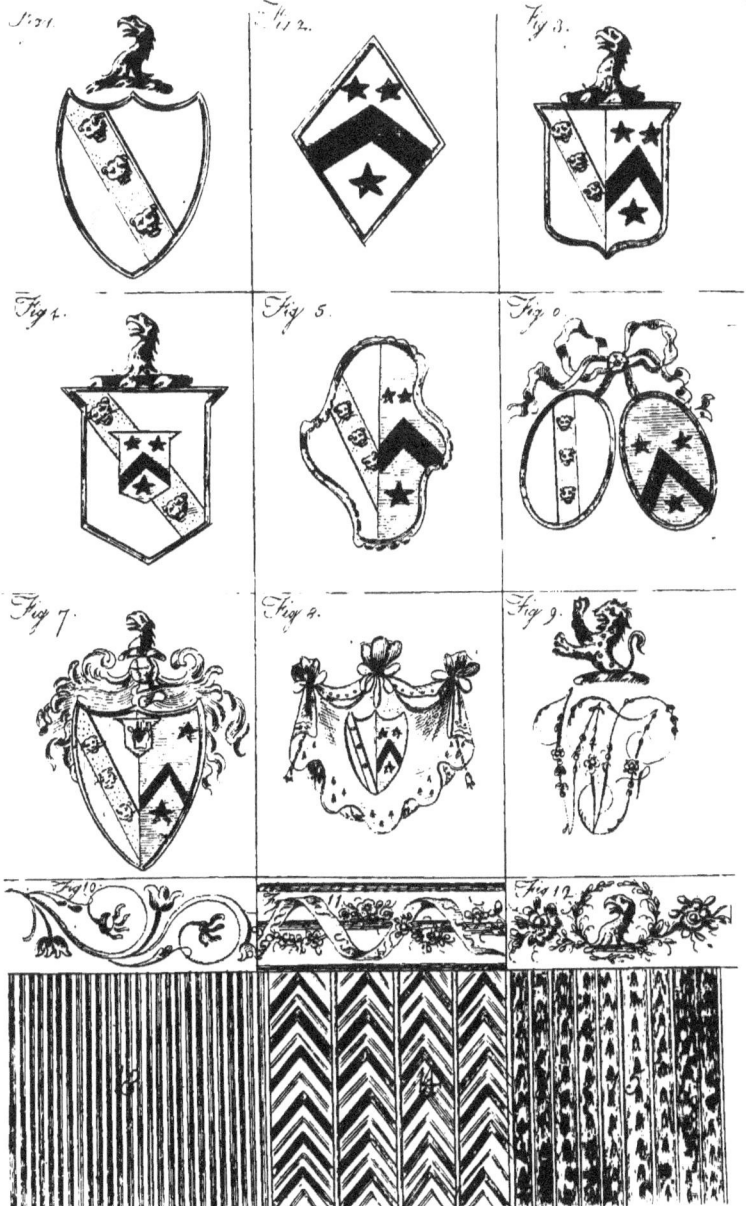

PAINTING, VARNISHING, &c.   197

Fig. 4. The manner in which the lady's arms are to be borne, if the lady is an heirefs, which is in a feparate fhield, within the centre of the hufband's, called a fcutcheon of pretence.

Fig. 5. The form of the fhield, called a widow's lozenge, in which either of the arms are to be placed, if the hufband dies.

Fig. 6. Two ovals, in which the arms are feparately placed, but not if the lady is an heirefs; the arms muft then be borne in a fhield, or oval, with the lady's arms in the middle: there is no rule for any form of fhield, whether round, oval, or cornered, makes no difference for a gentleman's arms; but, for a lady's, the form of a lozenge is the rule, except when married and empalled.

Fig. 7. The fcroll ornament, or a foliage mantle, which furrounds the arms or creft, inftead of the curtain mantles. Within the arms is the bloody hand which diftinguifhes a baronet.

Fig. 8. The mantle, of which there are various fhapes, is introduced only as an ornament to contain the arms or creft; it is a very ancient fafhion, continually fluctuating in form and fize, but is now reviving of an increafed fize to what it has been.

Fig. 9. A cypher and creft, which, either together or feparate, are often painted on a carriage inftead of the arms, or on the fide pannels or ſtyles, when the arms are on the door and ends; the creſt muſt be in its proper colour, but the cypher ſhould be a contraſt from the ground colour.

Fig. 10. A border of a neat pattern, which is ſpread wide, and fills the ſpace allotted to it with a good effect; this is not crowded with work, and may be conſidered one of the plaineſt.

Fig. 11. A border more enriched than the other, having alſo a fillet on each ſide; this may be conſidered of the middling. kind.

Fig. 12. A border filled with ſwags of flowers, having the creſt painted at about the diſtance of every ſix inches; this may be conſidered of the ſuperior kind.

Fig. 13. The ſtriping, which is ſometimes painted on the pannels to ornament them.

Fig. 14. The ſtriping and zig-zag work, which is alſo ſometimes painted on the pannels. .

Fig. 15. The ſtriping richly ornamented with huſk between: either pattern may be painted perpendicular or horizontal, as fancy may direct; the expence is the ſame either way; the cloſeneſs of the ſtripes and ornaments proportion the price, but ſhould be ſo cloſe that the ground colour be half covered with pencil-work.

PRICES

PRICES OF PAINTING.

WITH the painting of a carriage, the varnishing and japanning are included in the price, though frequently divided by some, to sanction a greater charge. What is properly an additional expence, is the ornament and heraldry work, as also the polished or high varnish and picking out.

It is frequently necessary to varnish or japan, separate from the painting, in consequence of a failure; but this is particularly mentioned under the subject of repairs in the Supplement.

The ornament painting cannot be reduced to any determinate price; being of various fanciful designs, it entirely depends on the quantity and merit of the work. The arms and crests, also the mantles which contain them, are, in general, tolerably regular in their prices, having nearly the same work in one pattern as another; but, when mantles are much furled, or arms much quartered, an increase of expence must be expected; as also when above the ordinary size, which is from three inches to four and a half for the arms, and from five to seven for the mantles; but the prices for the generality of painting may be nearly understood from the representation in the plate, describing each pattern as of three sizes, and proportioning the prices at so much per foot long; the striping to be charged by the foot square.

PRICES OF PAINTING BODIES AND CARRIAGES.

BODIES.	Coach. £ s. d.	Chariot. £ s. d.	Large Phaeton. £ s. d.	Middle-sized Phaeton. £ s. d.	Small Curricle. £ s. d.	Half-pannel Whiskey. £ s. d.	Cane Whiskey. £ s. d.
Painting and plain varnishing	3 0 0	2 10 0	2 0 0	1 18 0	1 15 6	1 10 0	0 18 6
Picking out the mouldings	0 10 6	0 10 6	0 7 6	0 7 0	0 7 6	0 7 0	0 7 0
Japanning the roof, quarters, and sword-case of coach and chariot, the doors and sword-case of phaetons, &c.	2 10 0	2 2 0	0 10 0	0 10 0	0 10 6	0 16 0	0 10 6
Polishing the pannels	2 10 0	2 2 0	0 1 0	0 1 3	0 5 6	0 1 0		
High varnishing ditto	5 15 6	4 4 0	3 3 0	3 3 0	3 3 6	2 10 0		
CARRIAGES.							
Plain painting and japanning the boots and budgets	2 2 0	2 2 0	1 15 0	1 11 0	1 7 6	1 1 0	1 1 0
Picking out the mouldings, one colour	1 1 0	1 0 0	0 18 0	0 15 0	0 12 6	0 10 0	0 10 0
Ditto, two colours, lining the mouldings with stripes	1 15 0	1 15 0	1 11 6	1 10 0	1 4 0	0 18 0	0 18 0
Ditto, three colours, or pannelling and much ornamented with stripes	2 10 0	2 10 0	2 5 0	2 0 0	1 10 6	1 5 0	1 5 0
Oil varnishing the carriage after finished with paint	0 15 0	0 15 0	0 15 0	0 15 0	0 10 6	0 10 0	0 10 0

PRICES OF PAINTING

This ſtatement will anſwer for the new painting of old bodies and carriages, by deducting one-fourth from the value of the firſt ſum for plain painting and japanning—for example:

	£.	s.	d.		£.	s.	d.
A new coach body painting is	3	0	0	An old one	2	5	0
Ditto japanning	2	10	0	ditto	1	17	6
Carriage painting	2	2	0	ditto	1	11	6

All the other charges are the ſame.

PRICES OF ORNAMENT AND HERALD PAINTING.

	Large.			Middle.			Small.		
	£.	s.	d.	£.	s.	d.	£.	s.	d.
A ſingle coat of arms to either pattern in the Plate	0	10	0	0	7	0	0	5	0
A pair of ſupporters	2	2	0	1	11	6	1	1	0
A creſt	0	5	0	0	4	0	0	3	0
A ditto, with a duke's, earl's, or baron's coronet	0	10	0	0	8	0	0	6	0
A cypher of one letter	0	3	0	0	2	6	0	2	0
A ditto of two letters	0	4	6	0	3	6	0	2	6
A ditto of three letters	0	5	0	0	4	0	0	3	0
A mantle of the uſual pattern	0	10	6	0	7	6	0	5	0
A ditto much furled	0	15	0	0	12	0	0	10	0

	Inch. wide.	Rich.			Middle.			Plain.		
Borders, per foot long	5	0	10	0	0	7	6	0	5	0
	4	0	7	6	0	6	0	0	4	0
	3	0	6	0	0	4	6	0	3	6
	2	0	4	6	0	3	6	0	2	6
	1¼	0	3	6	0	2	6	0	1	6
Fillets ditto	1	0	2	6	0	1	9	0	1	0
	¼	0	1	9	0	1	0	0	0	9
	½	0	1	0	0	0	9	0	0	6
Striping on pannels, per foot ſquare		0	10	0	0	7	6	0	5	0

CHAP.

CHAP. XV.

CHAISE HEADS, WINGS, KNEE-BOOTS, AND DASHING LEATHERS.

THOSE are conveniencies not all regularly used with every kind of carriage; but there are no phaetons or chaises finished without one or the other, which makes it necessary to describe them separately, that the proprietor of a carriage may chuse either, as is best suited to his inclination.

SECT. 1.

CHAISE HEADS.

PLATE XX.

HEADS to phaetons or chaises, &c. are found great conveniencies for sheltering from the sun, wind, or rain; and, excepting to very light carriages, ought not to be dispensed with. The principal

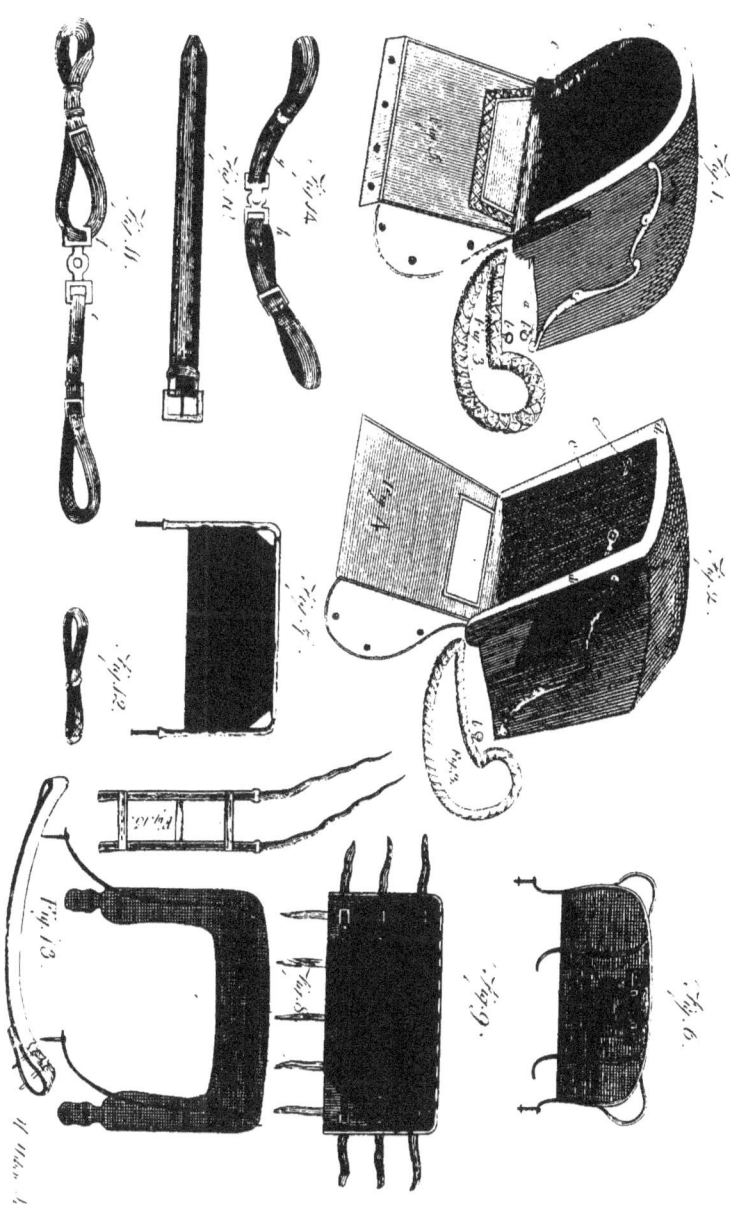

principal objections to them are, the additional weight of themselves, besides impeding the draught, if oppofite to the wind; but one great advantage in them is the eafe they can be removed with, according to the expectation of the weather. They are of two different forms, and are furnifhed with different conveniencies; but are all made as is defcribed in Plate v. with light wooden ribs, which are afterwards covered with a grained leather, and lined with woollen, ferge, or broad cloth, the fame as the body is lined with. The cloth is the preferable lining, though ferge is often fubftituted in its place.

Fig. 1. Reprefents a round or waggon-head, made on an iron frame *a a*, by which means it is eafily removed, when the wings are to be ufed, which are fecured by the fame fixtures *b b* as the head is. The infide is furnifhed with two curtains *e e*; the narroweft is hung on the driving fide, for freedom to the driver; the wideft is to fhelter the other paffenger.

Fig. 2. Reprefents a fquare head, with conveniencies on the infide at *c c* to fet and refet the head, without the trouble of reaching over to put up or down the joints, from the outfide, as ufual; the feams of the leather are fewed in welts, and round the front *d d* a broad ftripe of leather,

welted

welted on the edge, is nailed, which shelters the infide, and is called a vallent.

SECT. 2.

WINGS.

ARE fixed to the fides or elbows of the chaife bodies, when a head is not ufed; their ufe is to form a reft for the arm, and fhelter the paffenger from the dirt which fplafhes from the wheels; they are light iron frames, covered with leather, and lined with cloth and lace, to anfwer the lining, and are moftly ornamented round the outfides with a plated frame; to flight cheap-built carriages the wings are fometimes made of wood only.

Fig. 3. Are two wings, with different trimmings; they are made to fix at the points in fquare ftaples, and are fcrewed on the elbow-rails with ring-fcrews.

SECT. 3.

KNEE-BOOTS, OR APRONS,

ARE coverings for the knees of the paſſengers in a chaiſe or phaeton; they are made of a fine grain leather, the ſame as the head, and lined with linen or light woollen ſerge, with a flap made of the ſame materials as the lining, which turns over and ornaments the top; they are made to extend from the foot-board, to which they are fixed, to the top of the elbow in front, with cheeks ſewed and welted on the ſides, and are faſtened to buttons fixed on purpoſe for them.

At the top of ſome knee-boots, an iron-jointed rod is ſewed in the leather, which fixes in ſpring ſockets on the elbow-rail; the particular uſe of the rods is to ſupport the knee-boot ſtraight and free from the knee of the paſſenger, and to preſerve them from the chance of falling out by the violence of any jolt the carriage may meet with.

Fig. 4. A knee-boot made to fix on the foot-board, and to hitch on at the top with a ring or leather loop to a button; the rings are moſt convenient.

Fig. 5. A knee-boot, which takes off occaſionally, being only hitched on to buttons fixed

in

in the footboard, having alfo an iron frame at the top for fafety.

---

sect. 4.

DASHING OR SPLASHING LEATHERS,

ARE conveniencies made to fix on the fore part of a carriage, to prevent the dirt fplafhing againft the pannels or paffenger, and alfo to hide the pofteriors of the horfe.

They are iron frames of various forms, covered with leather, which is either dreffed in oil, or japanned; they are ornamental conveniencies now very generally ufed, in particular to curricles; the top ends are formed in loops, for the hands to be placed in, to affift the perfon getting up.

Fig. 6 A dafhing-leather for a curricle, having loops projecting out for the hand to affift getting up by, and ftays on the frame which fix on to the back-bar, and keep it fteady; on the infide is a leather pocket, for the purpofe of carrying lince-pins, &c.

Fig 7. A dafhing-leather for a one-horfe chaife carriage, having no back-ftay, or iron loops for the hand, the leather is cut out at the corners

corners of the frame to anfwer the fame purpofe; thofe are made much lighter than the others.

Fig. 8. A dafhing-leather for a poft-chaife carriage, which is made to fill the fpace between the fprings and the boot, which it is formed to the fhape of, and encompaffes, having at the back long ftays, which help to fupport it; when the common coach-box is taken off, thofe are made to fix in its place.

Fig. 9. A dafhing-leather for the body of a poft-chaife; this is not an entire frame, but only top and fides, round which the leather is fewed, and buckles to the bottom of the body; it is fixed on the fore main braces, with either bolts or buckles: this entirely preferves the front pannel from dirt, when travelling on wet roads.

PRICE OF HEADS, WINGS, KNEE-BOOTS, AND DASHING-LEATHERS.

WITH thofe conveniencies every thing is included in the price, except the plating; fo that the difference of any pattern may eafily be known; and the feparate amount of either, added to the former ftatements, will give the value of carriages when completed with either of them.

HEADS

PRICES OF HEADS, &c

HEADS.	Lined with Cloth.			Serge.		
	£.	s.	d.	£.	s.	d.
A plain fixed head, lined with cloth	10	0	0	8	10	0
A plain fixed round ditto, ditto	12	0	0	10	10	0
The joints to turn with infide wrenches	1	10	0			
A frame to take off the head occafionally	1	6	0			
A pair of curtains, bound with narrow lace	0	18	0	0	10	0
A pair of oil-fkin ditto, lined with linen	0	16	0			
A fmall back-light, without a plated frame	0	6	0			

WINGS.

	Large.			Middle.			Small.		
	£.	s.	d.	£.	s.	d.	£.	s.	d.
A pair of iron-framed wings trimmed with two-inch lace	1	15	0	1	12	0	1	10	0

KNEE-BOOTS.

	Large.			Middle.			Small.		
	£.	s.	d.	£.	s.	d.	£.	s.	d.
A knee-boot fixed on the foot-board	2	4	0	2	0	0	1	18	0
A ditto to take off occafionally	2	8	0	2	6	0	2	2	0
An iron-jointed frame	0	18	0	0	17	0	0	16	0

Silvered buttons, with which they are faftened, are included in the above price; the lace for the falls is confidered of two inches width.

DASHING.

DASHING LEATHERS.

	£.	s.	d.
A curricle dashing-leather, with stays,	2	10	0
A light chaise ditto, no stays	1	15	0
A post-chaise ditto, with stays	3	0	0
A post-chaise or coach body ditto with buckles	2	12	6
A pocket for either	0	5	0

CHAP. XVI.

BRACES, POLE-PIECES, &c.

PLATE XX.

ARE the leather ſtraps, of various ſizes, made up with buckles, and are what the body is hung and checked by.

SECT. 1.

MAIN BRACES.

Fig. 10. Are what the body hangs by; the ſize and thickneſs ought to be proportioned to the weight they are to ſuſtain: the breadth for a coach is two inches and three quarters; for a chariot, two inches and a half; a phaeton, two inches and a quarter; a chaiſe, or other light body, two inches: they are of two, three, or four ſtripes, faſtened together by four rows of ſewings, and are made up with large plated buckles.

SECT.

BRACES, POLE-PIECES, &c.

SECT. 2.

COLLAR BRACES.

Fig. 11. Are thofe that go round the perch or crane, and are buckled through a loop or ring, fixed to the bottom of the body, to check the motion fideways, and to confine it from ftriking againft the wheels. Thofe for heavy bodies are of a double thicknefs, but fingle ftripes to light bodies, fuch as phaetons or gigs, are fufficient. Some are fixed to the perch-loop as *e*, while others run through the loop as *f*, to take off occafionally. The breadth is in general an inch and three quarters.

SECT. 3.

CHECK BRACES.

Fig. 12. Are for the purpofe of checking the motion endways, placed at the four angles of the body, and are always of fingle ftripes of leather; on phaeton or chaife bodies, they fometimes crofs the angles for ornament only. The ufual fize is an inch and a half broad, but of different lengths.

SECT. 4.

SAFE BRACES.

Fig. 13. Are things but feldom ufed: their purpofe is to receive the body, if, by accident, the fprings, the loops, or fhackles fail. They are fixed to irons, which are placed to the four angles of the carriage, in the fame manner as the fprings are, and hang loofe under the body; they are very neceffary for travelling carriages; the ufual fizes is half an inch thick, and two inches and a quarter broad, and from ten to eleven feet long.

SECT. 5.

POLE-PIECES.

Fig. 14. Are the ftraps which couple the horfes to the pole, and are regulated by the fize and weight of the carriage; they are from one inch and three quarters to two inches and a quarter broad, and thick in proportion; they are fometimes fixed to the pole end, and are called French and Englifh pole-pieces; thofe that run through a loop at the pole end, to take off occafionally,

are

are the French pole-pieces, *b*, which are a preferable fort; the others fixed to the pole end, as *g*, are the English.

PRICE OF BRACES.

IT is frequently a rule to charge one general price for coach and another for chariot braces, including the buckles; but the moſt perfect method is to charge for the length of each per foot, and to add the price of buckles to the amount: there being many different ſizes of ſtraps for other uſes beſides braces, the value of any may be collected from this rule; there is alſo a difference to be made, if the braces are of a different thickneſs, for ſtrong, light, or common buſineſs; the middle ſize is what is moſtly uſed.

Inches wide.	$2\frac{3}{4}$		$2\frac{1}{2}$		$2\frac{1}{4}$		2		$1\frac{3}{4}$		$1\frac{1}{2}$	
	s.	d.	s.	d.	s.	d.	s.	d.	s.	d.	s.	d.
Strong for heavy travelling bodies	4	6	4	0	3	6	3	0	2	6	2	0
Common ſize	4	0	3	6	3	0	2	6	2	0	1	6
Light for phaetons	3	6	2	6	2	6	2	0	1	6	1	0
Single ſtripes of leather	2	0	1	9	1	6	1	3	1	0	0	9

The meaſure to be taken from the bridge of the buckle to the point of the ſtrap.

The lengths of coach and chariot braces are nearly the ſame with each other, which, in general, meaſure about four feet; ſo that, including

PRICE OF BRACES, &c.

the buckles with the braces, the usual prices charged for common braces are,

	Coach.			Chariot.		
	£.	s.	d.	£.	s.	d.
Main braces, with plated buckles, the set	4	4	0	3	13	6
Check braces, with ditto, the set	0	12	0	0	12	0
A pair of safe braces, with fixtures	4	4	0	3	13	6
Cross ditto, the pair	0	7	6	0	7	6
Single collar braces, with iron buckles, the pair	0	12	0	0	12	0
Double ditto, ditto	0	15	0	0	15	0
French pole-pieces, with polished buckles, the pair	1	6	0	1	4	0
English ditto	1	0	0	0	18	0
A set of point-straps and plated buckles for main braces	0	6	0	0	6	0

For *Price of Cradles*, see page 131.

CHAP.

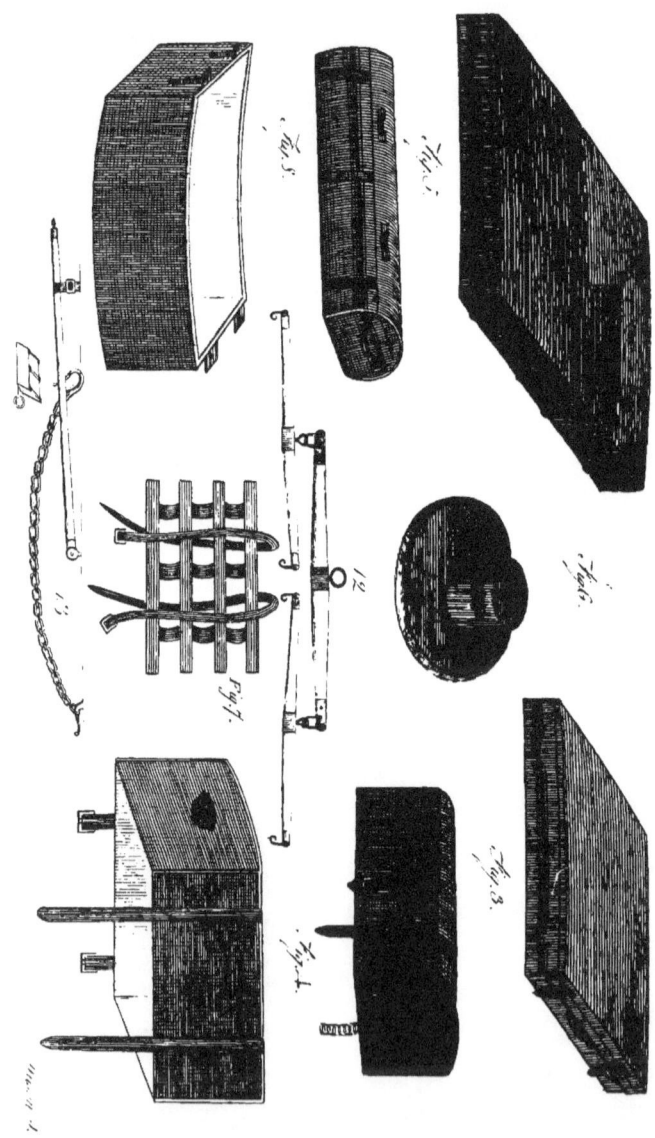

Plate XXI

CHAP. XVII.
TRAVELLING CONVENIENCIES.

PLATE XXI.

THERE are many conveniencies ufed with carriages, but more efpecially with thofe for travelling, that are not manufactured, but only fold and fitted by the coachmakers; the principal of which are, trunks, imperials, cap and hat boxes of various defcriptions; thofe things are ufually made of boards, covered with leather of two or three forts, in which there is a material difference: the beft leather is the ox hide, called neat's leather; but horfe hides are moft frequently ufed, and are fufficiently good for the purpofe: but an inferior leather is often fubftituted, which is not of one-fourth the value of the horfe-leather, though often impofed for it —this is fheep-fkin, commonly called bazil leather, which is of fo flender a texture, that it tears almoft like paper. For many light purpofes, fheep-fkin covered trunks will anfwer in place of a better leather, and a material faving of expence will be made.

SECT. 1.

TRUNKS.

Fig. 3. Trunks ufed for carriages are required to be made particularly ſtrong, and are moſtly ſtrengthened at the corners and joints with thin iron plates; the leather which covers them alſo adds to the ſtrength; they are uſually braſs nailed on the outſide, which is done to ornament and preſerve the leather from injury by rubbing; in particular, if covered with bazil leather: they are lined with paper or linen; the linen is to be preferred.

SECT. 2.

INSIDE STRAPS AND LATHS.

Fig. 7. Are conveniencies to confine what the trunk contains from ſhifting about: they are made with four or five laths, covered with cloth or paper, which are nailed at a ſmall diſtance from each other to three pieces of girth web, and lie at the top of the parcels within the trunk; on the

TRAVELLING CONVENIENCIES. 217

the bottom of the trunk ſtraps are nailed, which buckle round the laths, and keep all tight.

SECT. 3.

TRUNK COVERS.

Fig. 4. Theſe are made to fit the outſide of the trunks, which they cover and preſerve while in uſe; they are only made to cover thoſe trunks which are expoſed to the weather, and are uſually made of thick painted cloth, with holes at the ſides for the handles of the trunk to be got at.

SECT. 4.

TRUNK STRAPS AND BELTS.

Fig. 9 and 10. Are to confine and ſecure the trunk from ſhifting about, or from being ſtolen; the ſtraps are made of common thick leather of about an inch and a half broad, with an iron roller buckle. The chain-belt is a contrivance to fix round the trunk, which it locks to the platform; it is made of thin ſheet iron, jointed by wire
loops,

loops, and covered with thin leather, and is fecured by a padlock.

SECT. 5.

IMPERIALS.

Fig. 1 and 2. Thefe are large flat cafes, made to the form of the whole, or part, of the roof of the body; they are great conveniencies to carry light articles fafe, moftly defigned for apparel: they are made of light, thin deal boards, covered with neat's leather, and lined with linen; the bottom is lined with tow and baize, to prevent its rubbing the roof: if intended to cover the whole of the roof, they are moft convenient to remove, if divided into two parts; and, as the half is often fufficient for ufe, it faves unneceffary luggage. Of thofe things there is alfo a difference in the materials, and method of making. They are fixed on the roof by means of ftraps and ftaples, which are included with the imperials, in the prices ftated for them.

SECT. 6.

CAP BOX.

Fig. 5. A cap-box is a cafe made convenient for carrying ladies' head-dreſſes fafe; they are of a roundifh form, and are moſtly hung on the back of the body, refembling a fword-cafe; the lid is faftened fometimes in the manner of a portmanteau, or with a fingle lock; it is fixed on the back by means of thumb-fcrews and key-ſtaples; but, like the trunk, is made of different materials, according to the price.

SECT. 7.

HAT BOXES.

Fig. 6. A hat-box is a convenience for carrying hats, made of ſtout leather, in the exact form of a hat, opens at the bottom, and is fecured by a padlock; it is ufually faftened to the roof, or front budget of the carriage, with ſtraps.

SECT. 8.

WELLS.

Fig. 8. A well is a convenience ufed in travelling carriages for ſtowage; it is a ſtrong wooden caſe fixed on the bottom of the body with iron-work, ſo as to be occaſionally taken off, if deſired; the acceſs to it is from the infide of the body, having a trap-door in the bottom, under the carpet, and ſecured by a lock: if wells are made to bodies hanging on perch carriages, there muſt be two of them—one on each fide of the body, with the perch between them; they are lined with linen or baize, but painted black on the outſide.

SECT. 9.

SPLINTERS, OR SPLINTER-BARS,

Fig. 12. Are the ſhort bars which are hung to a hook at the end of a pole, when leading horſes are required: there are three uſed, hung to each other—the centre one hooks on the pole end, the other two hook on the ends of it: on each end
of

of the two out-fplinters, the traces of the harnefs are faftened; fometimes the traces of the leading harnefs are fixed to the collars of the wheel-harnefs, which method looks beft; but the draught is not fo equal as when drawn from fplinters: a fpare bar or two is always neceffary, in cafe of one breaking by a fudden pull of the horfe.

SECT. 10.

DRAG-CHAINS AND STAFF,

Fig. 13. Are neceffary to every travelling carriage; the chain is to lock the wheels, and to prevent the velocity of the carriage being too great when defcending a hill; the ftaff is to ftop the carriage, and to give reft to the horfes when afcending a hill; the chain is fixed to a hook about the middle of the perch or crane, with a hook or fhoe at the end for the wheels; the hook is moft handy for ufe, but the fhoe is preferable, as it preferves the iron of the wheel from injury, when dragging on hard, ftony ground; the chain being covered with leather prevents it from rattling; the drag-ftaff is fixed nearer the hind part of the carriage, with jointed iron-work, and is made of ftrong afh, with iron ferrules

ferrules on the ends, and a spike at the bottom, to make it hold secure in the ground; they are both fastened up with straps when out of use.

SECT. 11.

OILED COVERS TO THE BODY,

ARE to preserve the paint from the injury of the road-dirt, or boughs, while travelling: oil-skin covers are frequently used, and are so made that the doors may open and shut with the cover on; every part of the body, except the windows and bottom, is covered; it is made to fit to the exact form of the body, and looped on to small plated buttons, so as to be taken off occasionally; they are made of common oil linen, lined with a soft baize, and bound with a worsted tape.

SECT. 12.

SPRINGS CORDING.

THE purpose of cording springs is to prevent danger and delay, if by accident a plate should break, and also to strengthen them when required ed to be heavy loaded: to carriages that have heavy imperials, and much luggage in the body, it is very neceffary, which is done by placing a thin piece of afh, or a length of cord along the back, and afterwards twifting a fmall, but ftrong, cord round, and faftening it well at the top.

SECT. 13.

TOOL BUDGET,

IS a fmall convenience made to hang by ftraps under the hind part of a carriage, for the purpofe of carrying a few fpare bolts, nuts, lince-pins, nails, &c. with the few requifites for the coachman's ufe—fuch as a wrench, a hammer, a chiffel, a pair of pincers, &c. that in cafe of trifling accidents on the road, the defect may be fupplied without delay.

PRICE OF TRAVELLING REQUISITES.

IN the value of thofe things are included the painting, the ftraps, buckles, fcrews, bolts, &c. with which they are faftened.

TRUNKS.	Large.			Middle.			Small.		
	£.	s.	d.	£.	s.	d.	£.	s.	d.
Beft leather, welted or nailed, lined with cloth	3	13	6	3	0	0	2	2	0
Bazil leather, ditto, ditto, lined with paper	3	0	0	2	10	0	1	15	0
Infide ftraps and laths	0	6	0	0	5	0	0	4	0
TRUNK COVERS.									
Trunk covers made of neat's leather	2	5	0	1	15	0	1	1	0
Ditto made of oil or painted cloth	0	10	6	0	7	6	0	5	0

STRAPS AND BELTS.

	s.	d.
Straps and belts, 1¼ inch wide, iron buckles, at per foot	1	3
Chain belts, 1½ inch wide, with padlock, at ditto	2	9

IMPERIALS.	Beft.			Inferior.		
	£.	s.	d.	£.	s.	d.
A whole imperial for a coach roof	10	10	0	9	9	0
Two ditto for ditto	11	0	0	10	0	0
A fmall one for the middle only	5	15	6	5	0	0
A whole imperial for a chariot roof	7	7	0	6	10	0
Two ditto for ditto	7	17	6	7	0	0
A fmall one for ditto	4	10	0	4	0	0

CAP-BOX.

	£.	s.	d.	£.	s.	d.
A cap-box with faftenings complete	3	10	0	3	3	0

HAT-BOX.

	£.	s.	d.	£.	s.	d.
A hat-box with a padlock and two ftraps	2	12	6	2	5	0

WELLS.

PRICE OF TRAVELLING REQUISITES. 225

	Coach or Chariot.
WELLS.	£. s. d.
A large well for the body hanging on a crane-neck carriage — — —	2 12 6
Two small ditto for the body hanging on a perch carriage — — —	4 14 6

SPLINTER-BARS.

A set of splinter-bars complete — —	1 5 0
A main, or middle ditto — —	0 10 0
An end, or draught bar — —	0 7 6

CHAINS AND STAFFS.

A drag-chain, with hook — —	0 8 0
A drag-chain, with shoe — —	0 15 0
Covering the chain with leather —	0 4 0
A drag-staff — — —	0 10 6

OIL-COVERS.

	Coach.	Chariot.
	£. s. d.	£. s. d.
An oil-cover complete, with plated pins	5 10 0	4 10 0

	Coach or Chariot.
SPRINGS CORDING.	£. s. d.
Cording a set of springs — —	1 1 0

TOOL BUDGET.

A coachman's tool budget — —	0 10 6

Vol. I. Q CHAP.

CHAP. XIX.

HANGING OF BODIES.

THE bodies of carriages are fufpended from the fprings by braces; the proper method of executing this, adds much to the elegance of the carriage, and eafe of the paffengers; in particular in four-wheeled carriages, where the rule of hanging fhould be fuch as to be free from the obftruction of the fore wheels when turning, and without hanging too much within the hind wheels; and if on a crane-necked carriage, to obferve that a regular diftance be preferved between the crane and the bottom of the body, which fhould be hung fo as that the doors be directly perpendicular; but fafhion has introduced a method of hanging the bodies of coaches and chariots low behind, which has been followed to an extremity; the advantage of this method is certainly eafe to the rider, and to chariots it may be preferred on that account; but to coaches, it not only looks improper, but takes away the advantage of equal accommodation, by making one feat more eafy than the other.

To

HANGING OF BODIES.

To phaetons, gigs, or curricles, there are various methods of hanging, sometimes from braces at both ends, but are mostly from the hind end only, and that in different directions, from the springs to the bottom or middle of the body; the fore-end springs are often fixed to both body and carriage, and, being united at the ends, depend on their own elasticity for ease; if the hanging will admit a brace, however short, it is preferable; the springs with a brace round them, agreeable to the present fashion of hanging gigs or curricles, have the advantage for ease.

The placing of phaetons so forward as usual, is to give advantage to the driver over the horses, and to ease the draught, by bringing the weight forward; but does not look so well as if hanging between the wheels.

In all carriages, the body should be so hung as that the access to it may be no way obstructed by the wheels, which is frequently the case, particuly to one horse carriages.

END OF THE FIRST VOLUME.

A

PLAN

FOR

REGISTERING,

SO AS TO PURCHASE

CARRIAGES AND HORSES,

WITHOUT EXPENCE OR TROUBLE.

By WILLIAM FELTON, COACHMAKER,
No. 36, LEATHER-LANE, HOLBORN.
AND No. 254, OXFORD-STREET, NEAR GROSVENOR-SQUARE.

PLAN, &c.

THE inconveniencies gentlemen are expofed to, who attempt to buy or fell horfes or carriages on their own judgement, has induced W. FELTON to propofe to the public the following plan, whereby thofe impofitions fo commonly practifed may be avoided, and greater advantages derived than from any mode ever yet adopted.

Any

Any perſon, having either horſe or carriage to ſell, or wanting to purchaſe either, may be readily ſuited without trouble, expence, or riſk. Thoſe who want to ſell are to ſend in writing the particular deſcription with the price, where, and at what time, it is to be ſeen; which will be correctly copied, and inſerted in books kept for the purpoſe: and thoſe wanting to purchaſe, are alſo to ſend a deſcription of the things wanted, and references will be immediately given to thoſe likely to ſuit, ſo that principals meet, and treat with each other.

To make it more convenient, and alſo to facilitate the objects of this deſign, a regularly-printed catalogue will be publiſhed once a month, containing the various kinds of carriages and horſes wanted either to purchaſe or ſell; and, for the convenience of the public, one of thoſe of thofe catalogues will be left at the bar of each principal coffee-houfe in town. In the catalogue a minute defcription will be given, the proprietor's name and addrefs only omitted.

The hope of extending his bufinefs is the principal advantage W. FELTON expects to derive by this plan, as no charge whatever is made for trouble of regiftering, the expence of catalogues, referring, &c.—the only confideration he expects is from thofe who are fuited, by this means, with a carriage, to employ him to do the repairs, or make fuch alterations as may be found neceffary, which will be done agreeable to the prices he has publifhed; and thofe who fell, are to allow a commiffion of two and a half per cent. on the amount regiftered for, whether horfe or carriage; fo that, in fact, nothing is expected, if no benefit is derived. If called upon to attend, and purchafe for any one, or fet a value, two and a half per cent. on fuch valuation, or amount of purchafe, will be expected for his judgment and trouble. Not being a competent judge of horfes, he declines purchafing or valuing them on any confideration.

W. FELTON has been induced to revife his former plan, where money was taken for regiftering, to prevent others impofing on the public, who, for the expectations of the advanced money, has pirated his plan, and opened offices of the fame defcription; but the public muft be aware of the difadvantages of countenancing others, for by dividing the number regiftered, fo fair a chance of being fuited cannot be expected as if they were all contained in one lift.

CARRIAGES

CARRIAGES PRESERVED.

W. FELTON, wiſhing to make himſelf every way uſeful to the public, proffers his ſervices in this ſingular, but uſeful, plan.

Carriages are often as much injured by neglect as by uſe, and, for the want of proper care, often become an expenſive charge, and perſons riding in them are often expoſed to danger, for want of timely repairs.

To prevent thoſe inconveniencies, W. F. offers his ſervices to ſuperintend the care of them, without expecting any other intereſt than a ſmall annual charge for his trouble. He will attend at leaſt once a fortnight, on regular days, to examine the carriage, and fee if any repair is wanting; if it is properly taken care of; to direct what is neceſſary to be done; and to prevent that from being done which is not neceſſary. It is preſumed much advantage will be derived from the above plan; and any gentlemen who chuſe to countenance W. F. in it, are requeſted to ſend their names; as it will not be worth his attending without, at leaſt, 100 engagements. The only expence is One Guinea per year, half to be paid on the firſt attendance, and the other half at the end of the year. It is preſumed much will be faved, beſides the ſatisfaction of having the carriage well looked after, without the leaſt trouble to the proprietor in ſuperintending the care of them.

For

For the greater convenience of profecuting thofe plans to advantage, W. F. has opened two houfes, the one fituated No. 36, Leather-Lane, Holborn, near Liquorpond-Street; the other, No. 254, Oxford-Street, near Grofvenor-Square; where all letters directed, and poſt-paid, will be attended to.